F1
2003

C000184110

Fotografia / *Photography* / Fotografie	**BRYN WILLIAMS** - FRITS VAN ELDIK - PAOLO D'ALESSIO
Disegni tecnici / *Cutaways* / Illustrationen / *Illustraties*	**PAOLO D'ALESSIO**
Realizzazione grafica / *Graphic realization* / Grafische vormgeving	**DIEGO GALBIATI**
Traduzioni / *Translations* / Übersetzung / *Vertaling*	**JULIAN THOMAS** / **RICK WINKELMAN**
Stampa / *Printing* / Druck	**POLIGRAFICA ANTENORE** - PADOVA (ITALY)
Realizzazione / *Editorial production* / Herstellungskoordination / *Redactie en samenstelling*	© **2003 WORLDWIDE** / **SEP EDITRICE - CASSINA DE PECCHI** / **(MILANO - ITALY)** / WWW.SEPEDITRICE.COM

Member of the
World Sportpublisher's Association

Printed in Italy - October 2003

© 2003 SEP Editrice - Cassina de Pecchi (Milano - ITALY)
ISBN 88-87110-41-7

© 2003 North American Edition - Voyageur Press - Stillwater, MN
ISBN 0-89658-032-6 - ISSN 1527-5337

© 2003 Nederlands Taalgebied Ars Scribendi BV - Harmelen
ISBN 90-5566-009-4

© 2003 Race Report - Hilversum
ISBN 90-5566-011-6

Si ringrazia
AUTOSPRINT
settimanale di automobilismo sportivo leader in Italia,
fonte inesauribile di informazioni e dati statistici ripresi per questo libro.

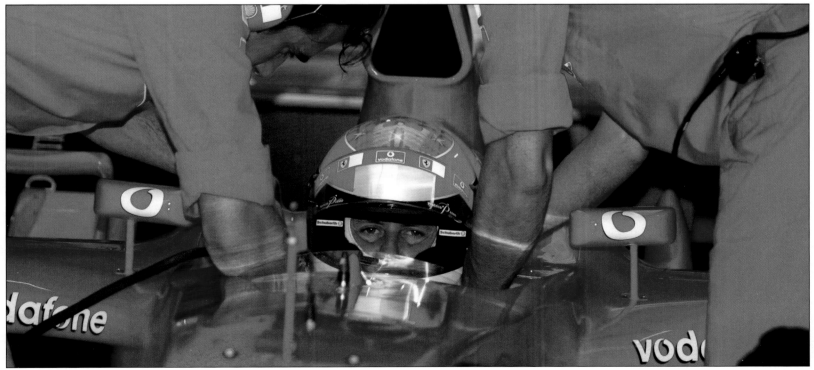

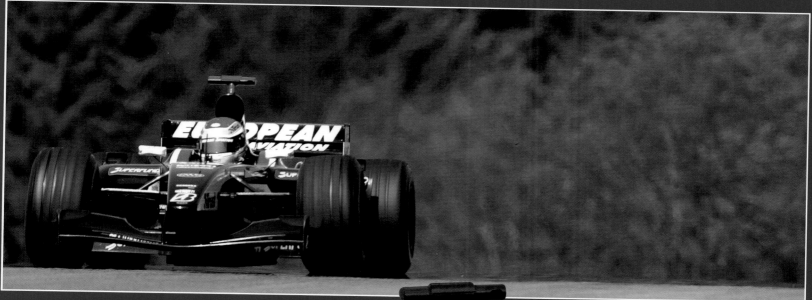

DIP

OIL

$+$

OC

MIX

SHIFT

VOL

REV
~~~~~~

NEUTRAL

PIT CONFIRM

AUTOSHIFT

Off	OFF	1
N N	EBrk	2
+ +	12b	3
- ++	12B	4
sm	10b	5
sm	10B	6
m	8b	7
t	8B	8

FiA 7998

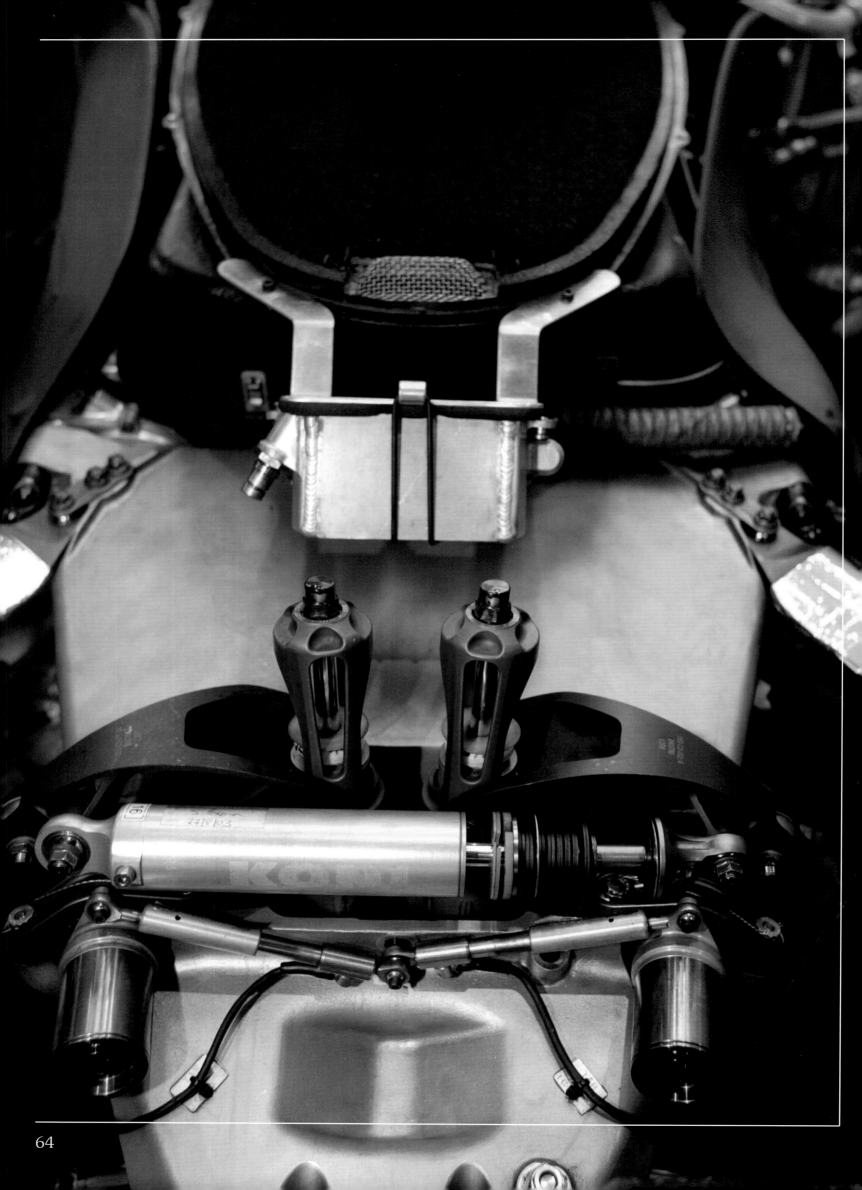

**Michael
SCHUMACHER**

**Rubens
BARRICHELLO**

**Juan-Pablo
MONTOYA**

**Ralf
SCHUMACHER**

**Kimi
RAIKKONEN**

**David
COULTHARD**

**Fernando
ALONSO**

**Jarno
TRULLI**

**Jenson
BUTTON**

**Jacques
VILLENEUVE**

**Cristiano
DA MATTA**

**Olivier
PANIS**

**Heinz-Harald
FRENTZEN**

**Nick
HEIDFELD**

**Giancarlo
FISICHELLA**

**Ralph
FIRMAN**

**Mark
WEBBER**

**Antonio
PIZZONIA**

**Jos
VERSTAPPEN**

**Justin
WILSON**

Michael Schumacher

Date of birth: 3 January 1969, Hurt-Hermulheim (Germany)
F1 debut: Belgian GP 1991

Year	Team	GP	Points	Pole	Victories
1991	Jordan/Benetton-Ford	6	4	-	-
1992	Benetton-Ford	16	53	-	1
1993	Benetton-Ford	16	52	-	1
1994	Benetton-Ford	14	92	6	8
1995	Benetton-Renault	17	102	4	9
1996	Ferrari	15	59	4	3
1997	Ferrari	17	78	3	5
1998	Ferrari	16	86	3	6
1999	Ferrari	9	44	3	2
2000	Ferrari	17	108	9	9
2001	Ferrari	17	123	11	9
2002	Ferrari	17	144	7	11

Rubens Barrichello

Date of birth: 23 May 1972, Sao Paulo (Brazil)
F1 debut: Brazilian GP 1993

Year	Team	GP	Points	Pole	Victories
1991					
1992					
1993	Jordan-Hart	16	2	-	-
1994	Jordan-Hart	15	19	1	-
1995	Jordan-Peugeot	17	11	-	-
1996	Jordan-Peugeot	16	14	-	-
1997	Stewart-Ford	17	6	-	-
1998	Stewart-Ford	15	4	-	-
1999	Stewart-Ford	16	21	1	-
2000	Ferrari	17	62	1	1
2001	Ferrari	17	56	1	-
2002	Ferrari	17	77	3	4

David Coulthard

Date of birth: 27 March 1971, Twynholm (Scotland)
F1 debut: Spanish GP 1994

Year	Team	GP	Points	Pole	Victories
1991					
1992					
1993					
1994	Williams-Renault	8	14	-	-
1995	Williams-Renault	17	49	5	1
1996	McLaren-Mercedes	16	18	-	-
1997	McLaren-Mercedes	17	36		2
1998	McLaren-Mercedes	16	56	3	1
1999	McLaren-Mercedes	16	48	-	2
2000	McLaren-Mercedes	17	73	2	3
2001	McLaren-Mercedes	17	65	2	2
2002	McLaren-Mercedes	17	41	-	1

Kimi Raikkonen

Date of birth: 17 October 1979, Espoo (Finland)
F1 debut: Australian GP 2001

Year	Team	GP	Points	Pole	Victories
1991					
1992					
1993					
1994					
1995					
1996					
1997					
1998					
1999					
2000					
2001	Sauber-Petronas	16	9	-	-
2002	McLaren-Mercedes	17	24	-	-

Juan Pablo Montoya

Date of birth: 20 September 1975, Bogotà (Colombia)
F1 debut: Australian GP 2001

Year	Team	GP	Points	Pole	Victories
1991					
1992					
1993					
1994					
1995					
1996					
1997					
1998					
1999					
2000					
2001	Williams-BMW	17	31	1	1
2002	Williams-BMW	17	50	7	-

Ralf Schumacher

Date of birth: 30 June 1975, Hurt-Hermulheim (Germany)
F1 debut: Australian GP 1997

Year	Team	GP	Points	Pole	Victories
1991					
1992					
1993					
1994					
1995					
1996					
1997	Jordan-Peugeot	17	13	-	-
1998	Jordan-Mugen	16	14	-	-
1999	Williams-Supertec	16	35	-	-
2000	Williams-BMW	17	24	-	-
2001	Williams-BMW	17	49	1	3
2002	Williams-BMW	17	42	-	1

Nick Heidfeld

Date of birth: 10 May 1977, Monchengladbach (Germany)
F1 debut: Australian GP 2000

Year	Team	GP	Points	Pole	Victories
1991					
1992					
1993					
1994					
1995					
1996					
1997					
1998					
1999					
2000	Prost-Peugeot	16	-	-	-
2001	Sauber-Petronas	17	12	-	-
2002	Sauber-Petronas	17	7	-	-

Heinz-Harald Frentzen

Date of birth: 18 May 1967, Monchengladbach (Germany)
F1 debut: Brazilian GP 1994

Year	Team	GP	Points	Pole	Victories
1991					
1992					
1993					
1994	Sauber-Mercedes	15	7	-	-
1995	Sauber-Ford	17	15	-	-
1996	Sauber-Ford	16	7	-	-
1997	Williams-Renault	17	42	1	1
1998	Williams-Mecachrome	16	17	-	-
1999	Jordan-Mugen	16	54	1	2
2000	Jordan-Mugen	17	11	-	-
2001	Jordan-Prost	15	6	-	-
2002	Arrows	12	2	-	-

Giancarlo Fisichella

Date of birth: 14 January 1973, Roma (Italy)
F1 debut: Australian GP 1996

Year	Team	GP	Points	Pole	Victories
1991					
1992					
1993					
1994					
1995					
1996	Minardi-Ford	8	-	-	-
1997	Jordan-Peugeot	17	20	-	-
1998	Benetton-Playlife	16	16	1	-
1999	Benetton-Playlife	16	13	-	-
2000	Benetton-Playlife	17	18	-	-
2001	Benetton-Renault	17	8	-	-
2002	Jordan	16	7	-	-

Ralph Firman

Date of birth: 20 May 1975, Norfolk (England)
F1 debut: Australian GP 2003

Jacques Villeneuve

Date of birth: 9 April 1971, St-Jean-sur-Richelieu (Canada)
F1 debut: Australian GP 1996

Year	Team	GP	Points	Pole	Victories
1991					
1992					
1993					
1994					
1995					
1996	Williams-Renault	16	78	3	4
1997	Williams-Renault	17	81	10	7
1998	Williams-Mecachrome	16	21	-	-
1999	BAR-Supertec	16	-	-	-
2000	BAR-Honda	17	17	-	-
2001	BAR-Honda	17	12	-	-
2002	BAR-Honda	17	4	-	-

Jenson Button

Date of birth: 19 January 1980, Frome, Somerset (England)
F1 debut: Australian GP 2000

Year	Team	GP	Points	Pole	Victories
1991					
1992					
1993					
1994					
1995					
1996					
1997					
1998					
1999					
2000	Williams-BMW	17	12	-	-
2001	Benetton-Renault	17	2	-	-
2002	Renault	17	14	-	-

Jarno Trulli

Date of birth: 13 July 1974,
Pescara (Italy)
F1 debut: Australian GP 1997

Year	Team	GP	Points	Pole	Victories
1991					
1992					
1993					
1994					
1995					
1996					
1997	Minardi-Prost	14	3	-	-
1998	Prost-Peugeot	16	1	-	-
1999	Prost-Peugeot	15	7	-	-
2000	Jordan-Mugen	17	6	-	-
2001	Jordan-Honda	17	12	-	-
2002	Renault	17	9	-	-

Fernando Alonso

Date of birth: 29 July 1981,
Curitiba (Spain)
F1 debut: Australian GP 2001

Year	Team	GP	Points	Pole	Victories
2001	Minardi	-	-	-	-

Mark Webber

Date of birth: 27 August 1976,
Queanbeyan (Australia)
F1 debut: Australian GP 2002

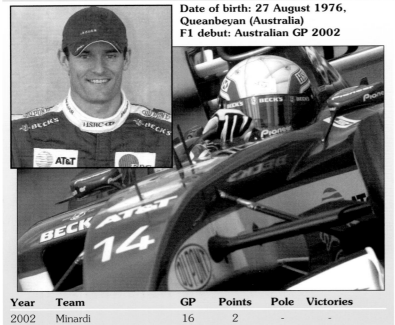

Year	Team	GP	Points	Pole	Victories
2002	Minardi	16	2	-	-

Antonio Pizzonia

Date of birth: 11 September 1980,
Manaus (Brazil)
F1 debut: Australian GP 2003

Olivier Panis

Date of birth: 2 September 1966,
(France)
F1 debut: Brazilian GP 1994

Year	Team	GP	Points	Pole	Victories
1991					
1992					
1993					
1994	Ligier-Renault	16	9	-	-
1995	Ligier-Mugen	17	16	-	-
1996	Ligier-Mugen	16	13	-	1
1997	Prost-Mugen	10	16	-	-
1998	Prost-Peugeot	15	-	-	-
1999	Prost-Peugeot	16	2	-	-
2000					
2001	BAR-Honda	17	5	-	-
2002	BAR-Honda	17	3	-	-

Cristiano Da Matta

Date of birth: 19 September 1973,
Belo Horizonte (Brazil)
F1 debut: Australian GP 2003

Jos Verstappen

Date of birth: 4 March 1972, Montfort (The Netherlands)
F1 debut: Brazilian GP 1994

Year	Team	GP	Points	Pole	Victories
1991					
1992					
1993					
1994	Benetton-Ford	10	10	-	-
1995	Simtek-Ford	4	-	-	-
1996	Footwork-Hart	16	1	-	-
1997	Tyrrell-Ford	17	-	-	-
1998	Stewart-Ford	9	-	-	-
1999	-	-	-	-	-
2000	Arrows	17	5	-	-
2001	Arrows-Asiatech	17	1	-	-
2002	-	-	-	-	-

Justin Wilson

Date of birth: 31 July 1978, Sheffield (England)
F1 debut: Australian GP 2003

Nicolas Kiesa

Date of birth: 3 March 1978, Copenhagen (Denmark)
F1 debut: German GP 2003

Zsolt Baumgartner

Date of birth: 1 January 1981, Budapest (Hungary)
F1 debut: Hungarian GP 2003

Marc Gene

Date of birth: 29 March 1974, Sabadell (Spain)
F1 debut: Australian GP 1999

Year	Team	GP	Points	Pole	Victories
1999	Minardi	16	1	-	-
2000	Minardi	17	-	-	-

Takuma Sato

Date of birth: 28 January 1977, Tokyo (Japan)
F1 debut: Australian GP 2002

Year	Team	GP	Points	Pole	Victories
2002	Jordan	17	2	-	-

F1 CALENDAR - 2003

March 7

Gerhard Berger leaves his job as head of BMW Motorsport, officially to devote more time to his transport firm and his family.

March 7

The new Minardi is launched in Melbourne's Federation Square by Paul Stoddart and the two drivers. Like last year the team can count on the presence of Australia's sexiest model, Sarah Jane, but Giancarlo Minardi is conspicuous by his absence.

March 7

Justin Wilson launches the first 'driver participation fund' in Formula 1. The aim is to put together 1.8 million Euro, the cost of a season of racing for Minardi.

March 9

This year's championship gets underway without one of the most popular drivers in Formula 1, Eddie Irvine. After 10 seasons in F1, which included 146 races and 4 wins for Ferrari in 1999, and 26 podium finishes, the Irish driver decided to call it a day.

March 9

Ferrari fails to make the podium for the first time since the European GP at the Nurburgring. Their successful run extended to 53 races, and included 35 wins: 29 for Schumacher, 5 for Barrichello and 1 for Irvine.

March 9

Two years after returning to Formula 1, Michelin take all three podium places for the first time with Coulthard, Montoya and Raikkonen.

March 9

First Formula 1 points for Spain's Fernando Alonso, who finishes seventh overall in Australia.

March 9

Olivier Panis sets fifth quickest time for Toyota on the start grid, the best result ever for the Japanese team. Unfortunately the French driver has to retire after 31 laps.

March 9

Four drivers make their Formula 1 debut in 2003:

Antonio Pizzonia (Jaguar)
Born in Manaus (Brazil) on September 11th 1980. Moved to England in 1997 to take part in the Formula Vauxhall Junior championship. Won the title the following year, becoming the youngest and first foreign driver to take the crown. In 2000 was British Formula 3 champion, with three wins and six podiums. Williams tester in 2001, and was so impressive that during a test at the Barcelona circuit last year his Jaguar bosses offered him a contract as factory driver in 2003.

Justin Wilson (Minardi)
Born in Sheffield (England) on July 31st 1978. In 1999 debuted in the FIA F3000 championship with Team Astromega, switching to Nordic Racing the following year. His successes include F3000 champion in 2001 with 3 wins, 2 pole positions and 10 podiums in 12 races with Nordic Racing. Wilson is the tallest driver in F1, which has created a few problems for Minardi in adapting the seat and pedals to his 1.92 m height.

Ralph Firman Jr. (Jordan)
Born in Norwich (England) on February 20th 1975. His career took off in Formula Nippon where he made his debut in 1997, becoming 2002 champion with Team Nakajima. Owes his arrival in F1 to his team manager, the first Japanese driver in the history of F1 (1987 with Lotus) who has close links with engine supplier Honda. Like Wilson, has a few problems fitting into the cockpit due to his 'vital statistics' (78 kg, 1.85 m).

Cristiano Da Matta (Toyota)
Born in Belo Horizonte (Brazil) on September 19th 1973. Brazilian Formula 3 champion in 1993 and Formula 3 champion in 1994. In 1997 moved to the USA to take part in the Indy Lights championship, winning 3 races and setting 1 pole position. Was also 'Rookie of the Year'. The following year he was crowned Indy Lights champion. Moved up into CART in 1999, winning the championship in 2002 with 7 victories and 7 pole positions.

March 23

First career win for Raikkonen, 23 years old from Finland, in his 35th race and first podium for Alonso, the youngest driver ever to finish in the top 3. The previous record belonged to Bruce McLaren, who finished third in the 1959 British GP.

April 6

Barrichello's Brazilian jinx continues (10 retirements in 11 races and a fourth place for Jordan-Hart in his second year in F1 in 1994).

April 6

Raikkonen first and Fisichella second at the chequered flag after a 55-lap rain shortened race. On April 11, after an FIA meeting in Paris, the order was changed to Fisichella first, followed by Raikkonen. First win for Fisichella after 110 GPs. The last time an Italian driver won a F1 race was 11 years ago: Patrese (Williams) in the 1992 Japanese GP.

April 14

Sauber sign as test-driver 19 year-old Swiss driver Neel Jani, currently taking part in Formula Renault V6.

April 18

Giancarlo Fisichella receives the Brazilian GP winner's trophy from Kimi Raikkonen at Imola, following an FIA ruling in Paris.

April 20

The CEA fire-fighters were present at Imola with an impressive organisation, including more than 200 specialists, the famous "CEA Lions", backed up by 33 special vehicles and more than 400 fire-extinguishers.

April 20

Jarno Trulli celebrates his 100th GP at Imola on an unlucky day which saw the Italian finish 13th after starting 16th on the grid.

April 20

Elisabeth Schumacher, Michael and Ralf's mother, died a few hours before the start of the race. She had been in a Cologne hospital for the last ten days. The two drivers returned from Germany to line up on the grid for the race. Michael went on to win while Ralf finished in fourth place.

May 4

The Ferrari F2003-GA makes its debut in Spain; Michael Schumacher sets pole and takes the win while Barrichello puts in the fastest lap.

May 11

During the CART race, Alex Zanardi returned to the Lausitzring, the scene of his horrific crash in 2001. Amidst the cheers of the fans, Alex completed the famous final 13 laps of the race at an impressive speed of 313 kph, setting a time of 37.487 seconds which would have earned him fifth place on the starting-grid.

May 18

Frentzen has little to celebrate on his 36th birthday (37 year-old Frenchman Olivier Panis is the F1 veteran at 37 years of age) at the Austrian circuit after his Sauber fails to start due to a clutch problem.

May 18

The Schumacher brothers celebrate 100 races together in Austria. The first time they appeared on the same podium was Monza 1998.

May 20

Alejandro De Tomaso, born in Argentina but resident in Modena, Italy for over 50 years, died at the age of 74. In F1 the Ford Cosworth-engined De Tomaso made its debut in 1970 with the Frank Williams team. Driver Piers Courage lost his life that year in the Dutch GP at Zandvoort.

June 1

Ralf Schumacher is the only driver to score points in the first 7 races of the year. At Monte Carlo, he could only finish fourth despite starting from pole position.

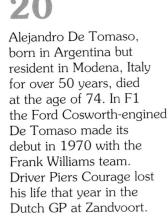

June 9

With a brief press release Ferrari made note that its sporting management team, made up of Jean Todt, Ross Brawn, Rory Byrne and Paolo Martinelli, has been reconfirmed until 2006. But the most eagerly awaited news for fans is that Michael Schumacher has also renewed his contract until the end of the 2006 season.

June 18

Paul Stoddart, Minardi's Australian owner, buys up most of the Arrows 2002 F1 stock after the team was wound up for bankruptcy.

June 27

Despite disappointing results this year, David Coulthard will probably be confirmed as McLaren driver in 2004. The Scot has been with McLaren since 1996.

June 29

Heinz-Harald Frentzen takes part in his 150th GP in the European GP at the Nurburgring. HH made his F1 debut in the 1994 Brazilian GP with the Mercedes-powered Sauber.

June 29

Williams and BMW announce that their partnership will continue until 2009. BMW made its debut in F1 in 1982 as engine supplier for Brabham with a 1400 bhp 1.5 litre turbo fitted to the BT50. They won the title the following year with Nelson Piquet.

July 20

British GP: For the first time ever in F1 history, a Toyota leads a grand prix race. Da Matta eventually finishes seventh.

July 4

In Friday qualifying for the French GP Minardi driver Jos Verstappen sets provisional pole thanks to the rain, which stopped falling during the Dutch driver's quick lap. Not a bad way to celebrate 100 races in F1!

July 23

From the German GP onwards Justin Wilson will probably take the place of Antonio Pizzonia at Jaguar while ex-F Ford, British F3 and F3000 driver, the 25 year-old Dane Nicolas Kiesa will probably make his debut for Minardi. Kiesa scored a clamorous win in the 2003 F3000 race at Monte Carlo when he overtook Bjorn Wirdheim on the line after the latter had slowed to celebrate the win with his mechanics on the pit-wall.

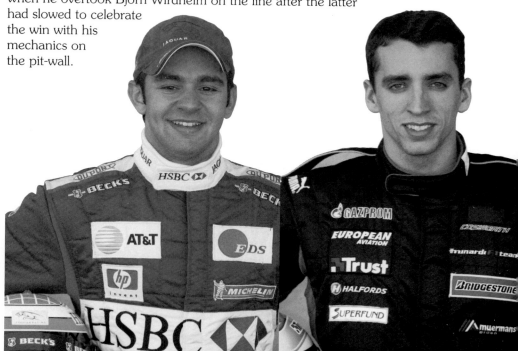

August 3

Toyota set another record in the German GP when the Japanese cars both finished in the points for the first time: 5th place for Panis and 6th for Da Matta.

August 3

Michelin also set a personal record at Hockenheim when the top six cars in the final standings were all on the French manufacturer's tyres for the first time ever.

August 8

The German architect Hermann Tilke presented the two new circuits that will be included in the 2004 championship calendar. The Shanghai circuit has a scheduled date of October 24, 2004 for the Chinese Grand Prix, while the Sakkir circuit is set to be the venue for the Bahrain Grand Prix on April 4, 2004.

CINA GP

BAHREIN GP

August 11

Tazio Nuvolari, considered by Enzo Ferrari to be the greatest driver of all time, died 50 years ago today. Born in 1892 in Castel d'Ario, province of Mantua, Nuvolari raced until 1950, first on motorbikes and then in cars. He took part in a total of 353 races, winning 105.

August 22

The McLaren driver line-up for 2004 was confirmed as David Coulthard and Kimi Raikkonen. This will be the ninth successive season for the Scottish driver in Ron Dennis's team.

August 24

Minardi, which made its F1 debut in the 1985 Brazilian GP, reached the 300 GP mark in Hungary.

August 24

Fernando Alonso scorse his maiden win in F1 in the Hungarian GP, which takes Renault back to the top of the winners' podium for the first time in 20 years. Their last win was in 1983 with Alain Prost at Zeltweg. Alonso also set two new records: the first Spanish driver to win in F1 and the youngest driver in history to win an F1 race.

September 14

The Monza win was Michael Schumacher's 50th for Ferrari and his fourth in the Italian GP.

October 11

After eight years in Formula 1, 132 races, and a world title in 1997 for Williams-Renault, Jacques Villeneuve was released from his contract with BAR just before the final race of the 2003 season. The Canadian's adventure in BAR, which was founded by his friend and manager Craig Pollock, began five years ago.

October 12

Celebrations in Ferrari for the fifth successive manufacturers' title which took the Italian team's haul to 13, and for Schumacher's fourth successive title with Ferrari after the two he won in 1994 and 1995 with Benetton.

THE 2003 SEASON

by Giorgio Stirano

It's that man Michael Schumacher again! Doubts had been cast at the start of the 2003 season over the German no longer being the champion of previous years and whether or not he had lost the hunger to win. Yet whenever he had the chance and was in a condition to do so, the five-times world champion proved that he had lost none of his determination.

The fact remains that if he had scored the same results in 2002 as he had this year, Michael Schumacher would have been in a condition to win the championship much earlier than the final round of the year, but the change in regulations in 2003 put paid to that idea.

The changes in qualifying for the starting-grid, now based on a Superpole one-lap dash, also helped to favour his rivals. In implementing these changes, the FIA gave the impression it was singling out the German driver and the Italian manufacturer for having been too successful over the past few years.

Although this was not the case, the FIA clearly had to try and keep Formula 1 as entertaining as possible and maintain interest high until the final rounds of the season. With the supremacy of Ferrari over the past few seasons, this idea had been a non-starter.

The changes to the scoring system, with 10 points going to the winner and just two less for the runner-up, helped to bunch up the standings right until the final round. Finnish driver Raikkonen, for example, was a championship contender despite winning fewer races than either Schumacher or Montoya.

The championship proved to be exciting right down to the wire and almost all the races were entertaining. The battle on the track was not due to the new regulations, but instead it was because Ferrari's rivals had finally succeeded in reaching the same competitive level as the Italian team, and in particular thanks to the efficiency of their Michelin tyres.

Ferrari had now become a shining example to all those teams that had worked hard over the winter to close the gap which had emerged throughout the 2002 season.

Williams had improved its chassis and aerodynamics package and BMW had increased the power and driveability of its engine, which during the previous season had already appeared to be the best on the grid.

Similar efforts had been made in McLaren, and the results proved to be just as efficient despite maybe not being as evident.

Behind the front-runners, Renault won the only race it had any real chance of winning, the Hungarian GP, with talented youngster, Alonso, while Toyota demonstrated that it was on the right path with a series of points-scoring finishes.

For its part, Ferrari was on the receiving end of some criticism: this was unworthy because the Maranello-based team won virtually half the races on the championship calendar.

Criticising the car and the team makes no sense whatsoever and it would be better to praise Ferrari's rivals who had finally reacted with decision and professionalism to the Italian team's domination.

Tyres had a major influence on the outcome of the championship. During the US GP it was clear how much tyre efficiency was fundamental for performance. The rain that slowly began to fall after the start caused problems for Schumacher who was unable to take the long fast banked curve at the same speed as his Michelin-shod rivals.

After the pit-stops, on a totally wet surface, Schumacher's intermediates were crucial in the German's annihilation of the opposition. While one wonders incessantly about this disparity in performance and how the tyre becomes 'the' fundamental component of the car, it becomes clear that tyre design is intrinsically linked with the functional characteristics of the car and vice-versa.

It has become a classic 'dog bites tail' situation. Ferrari has worked with Bridgestone for years while Williams and McLaren have more recently begun their collaboration with Michelin.

This year the two tyre manufacturers reached a similar performance level, but they did so in different conditions and circuits; and this is the reason for the alternating series of results throughout the year. Michelin tyres proved to be competitive in particularly severe weather conditions such as the torrid summer heat, whereas the Bridgestones worked well in more moderate climates.

Does tyre performance therefore depend on the weather? It would appear to be so, but to get a better idea, we should have a detailed look at how tyres are conceived.

A grand prix racing tyre is characterised as having a radial structure and a compound, which for simplicity's sake, we can call the part in rubber: its performance is the result of the behaviour of the structure in relation to the compound. From a technical point of view the design of a tyre represents an extremely complex problem because the 'framework' is made up of carbon and Kevlar fibres, arranged in such a way as to absorb vertical and lateral stress.

This stress brings about a constant elastic deformation which has an effect on the tyre tread, the area with which the tyre stays in contact with the ground. The combination of the behaviour of the structure, the compound and the atmospheric conditions lead the tyre tread to heat up to an approximate working temperature that oscillates between 100° and 150°. It is not advisable to go above or below these figures, because the tyre loses grip if the temperature is lower, or overheats if higher. This leads to a loss of grip due to the change in the chemical and physical composition of the compound, which degrades to a point where 'blistering' appears on the tread before the tyre collapses completely.

The two manufacturers have different philosophies in the way a tyre structure is conceived and in the construction of the compound and as a result their products (which last between 100 and 150 kms!) are influenced by these elements, which in turn have an effect on the general performance of the car and the driver.

The battle between the two tyre manufacturers has added extra excitement and interest to the 2003 season, making the outcome for the Drivers' and Constructors' title much more open and uncertain than in previous years.

Giorgio Stirano

HANS®
Head and Neck Support

The HANS® device was made compulsory in Formula 1 this year after several drivers had tried it out or even worn it in 2002.

Invented in the mid-1980s by Professor Robert Hubbard of Michigan State University, the HANS® (Head and Neck Support) safety system has been used in other categories of motor racing for a number of years and in particular in the CART, IRL and NASCAR series in the USA.

In 1997, with the collaboration of DaimlerChrysler and the FIA, Hubbard starter to develop a model for Formula 1, which was smaller and lighter than the original prototype.

In 2002 several F1 drivers volunteered to test the device. Some, including Heidfeld and Ralf Schumacher, were in favour while others such as Barrichello, Michael Schumacher and Montoya were against the system, not because of its efficiency but because it appeared to limit head motion when cornering.

The results of the test demonstrated that the device actually did reduce both neck stress during the race as well as the risk of serious injury in an accident.

The carbon-fibre/Kevlar collar system is worn on the upper body under the shoulder straps. It is connected to the helmet by two flexible tethers which allow normal head movement (left, right, up and down) but limit extreme head motion and neck load. Most drivers do not even realise it is there once they are wearing it, and as it is not connected to the vehicle in any way, they require no assistance in stepping out of the cockpit.

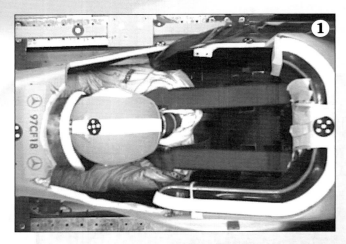

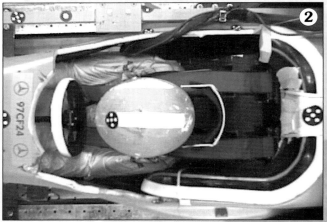

Photo **1** shows the movement of the driver's body in a front impact crash without the use of the HANS® safety device, while photo **2** shows the same impact with the system in use. Photo **3** and photo **4** show the same movement in a rear impact crash.

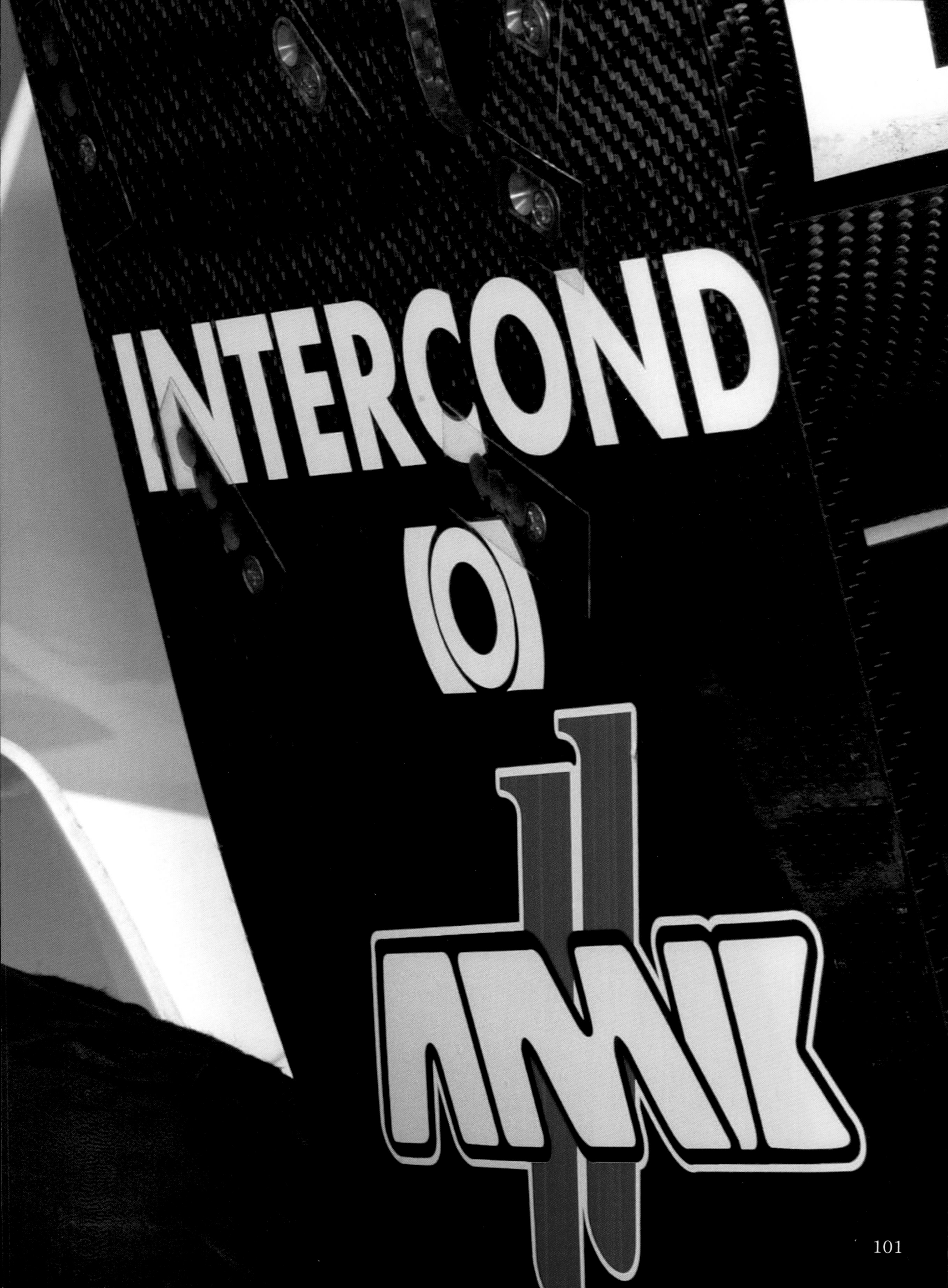
INTERCOND

F.1 2003: TRADING PLACES

By Paolo D'ALESSIO

The picture that emerged at the end of the 2002 Formula 1 season was alarming, to say the least. The season had gone into the archives with a fifth world title for Michael Schumacher and Ferrari winning 15 of the 17 races on the calendar, but above all with a worrying drop in spectator interest. The first people to realise this were Bernie Ecclestone, F1's undisputed boss, and the FIA, which immediately drew up a series of measures aimed at shaking up the top category of world motor sport: changes were made to the points-scoring system and qualifying (now one lap on Friday and Saturday), Sunday morning warm-up was abolished and the cars had to be recovered in parc fermé after Saturday qualifying and stay there until just before the start. The aim of this revolution was to make the races more uncertain, but also to limit the Ferrari domination that threatened to kill off all interest in the championship. It was vital to prevent the title race from being decided five or six rounds before the end, as in 2001 and 2002. At least that was the FIA's intention. One year on from the introduction of the new rules, all the problems of Formula 1 have clearly not been resolved. Let's take for example the much hoped-for reduction in costs. No one seems to have realised that more and more teams like Minardi, Jordan and Sauber are in difficulty, while the top teams (Ferrari, McLaren-Mercedes and Williams-BMW) are reckoned to have annual budgets of more than 500 million Euro. So much for cost cutting ...

Then came the matter of qualifying and parc fermé. A one-lap dash for pole, invented for television, might make the sponsors happy because they clearly benefit from TV coverage, but it has also brought about totally deserted grandstands on Friday and Saturday and a further drop in spectator numbers on race day. Not to mention parc fermé, which existed only on paper. The fear of having less than twenty cars on the starting-grid or the exclusion of the occasional top driver led to this rule being annulled and as a result accusations, suspicion and controversy. The rules are made to be respected however, even though they might not be the same for everyone.

The other element that sent Ferrari into a crisis in 2003 and rekindled the ambitions of Williams and McLaren was tyres; after their debacle in 2002, Michelin worked hard to make up lost ground over the winter and close the gap on Bridgestone. Michelin's improvement helped bring about Renault's return to the top twenty years after their last Formula 1 win. The final part of this technical analysis is in fact dedicated to the French manufacturer and to its history-making cars: from the first turbo engine, to the Renault-powered Williams and Benetton that dominated the world championship in the 1990s with Mansell, Prost, Schumacher, Damon Hill and Jacques Villeneuve.

FERRARI F2003 GA

Ferrari dedicated their new car to Giovanni Agnelli, who passed away just before its presentation and we are sure that 'L'Avvocato', as Agnelli was known, would have liked the F2003 GA. Not only did it win on the track, it was also one of the most beautiful Ferrari Formula 1 single-seaters in recent years, as well as one of the most refined cars ever built by the Maranello-based constructor. Rory Byrne, its designer, defined it as "... the most exasperated and innovative Ferrari of all time". Let's have a look in detail.

The F2003 GA represented a clear step forward from the car that dominated the 2002 world championship, but it was not a leap into the dark because it was a successful mixture of innovations and well-tried solutions. The aerodynamic package was one example. While the front was similar to the championship-winning F2002, with its 'anteater' nose and a curved front wing in the central part, the design of the sides and the rear was completely new. The sidepods were much smaller, curved at the front and tapered at the base. The real revolution in this area however was concealed inside the sidepods, and it was called fluid dynamics. The GA sported radiant masses that were smaller, more forward inclined and fan-shaped. This solution considerably reduced the front section and improved the Ferrari's performance right from its debut.

The intervention at the rear was just as radical, and the F2003 GA sported the most tapered rear end ever seen in Formula 1. Furthermore the periscope exhaust duct fairings, the so-called 'chimney stacks', were also made larger to speed up and further clean up the airflow over the rear wing. These were the major changes to the external appearance of the car, but there were also important innovations under the body-

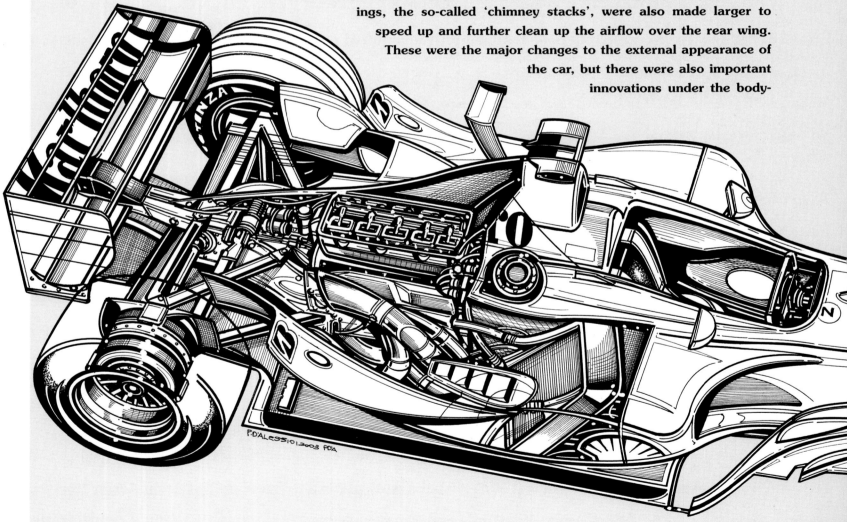

DESIGN: P. D'ALESSIO

work. The F2002's excellent chassis was made even lighter and linked to a brand-new suspension layout. At both the front and the rear, Ferrari engineers dusted off the pushrod-activated torsion spring layout in place of traditional helical springs and at the rear they even introduced new rotating shock absorbers.

The engine was the final piece in the 2003 jigsaw. Even though Maranello never releases official figures, the Ferrari 052 ten-cylinder engine was thought to produce more than 900 BHP of power, an extraordinary figure and one that was on the same level as the BMW V10 unit. Despite this and victory in its debut race, the F2003 GA did not dominate the season, as the two previous models had done in 2001 and in 2002.

The reason was that Ferrari's rivals had finally made up the engineering gap and also because the excellent GA was not without its defects. On more than one occasion it gave the impression of being a difficult car to set up, with unexpected reactions and clear limits; this was highlighted by the Bridgestone tyres, which were often in difficulty against the Michelins. In the middle of the season it looked like Ferrari was returning to past times, with its up-and-down performances and its tendency to enter into crisis on certain tracks.

Michelin had worked hard over the winter and in certain climatic conditions (i.e. warm weather!), the French manufacturer's tyres were up to a second a lap quicker than Bridgestone rubber. Coupled with the F2003 GA's defects, this created a few problems for Ferrari but it is in these circumstances that true champions emerge and Ferrari, after a disastrous summer, reacted in the best possible way by introducing a series of modifications to the car's aerodynamics package at the Italian Grand Prix. This, together with a super engine and some new Bridgestone tyres allowed Ferrari to turn around a season that had appeared to be compromised.

FERRARI F2003 GA

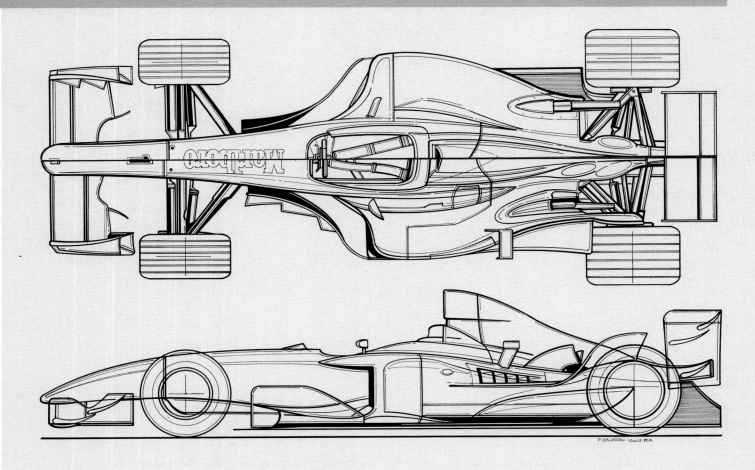

The design of the F2003 GA (below), compared with the car used last season and at the start of this season, shows the major aerodynamic differences between the two cars. The car dedicated to Gianni Agnelli is characterised by having smaller, more rounded sidepods and above all by a more accentuated tapering of the rear end. Note also the wide lateral deflectors, the extended 'chimney stacks', the periscope exhaust duct fairing and the design of the bargeboards.

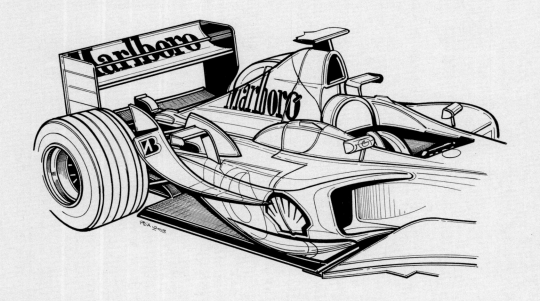

Ferrari's aerodynamics engineers also dug out the lower part of the sidepods and this modification, together with increased bodywork tapering helped to speed up the airflow over the rear and thus increase downforce.

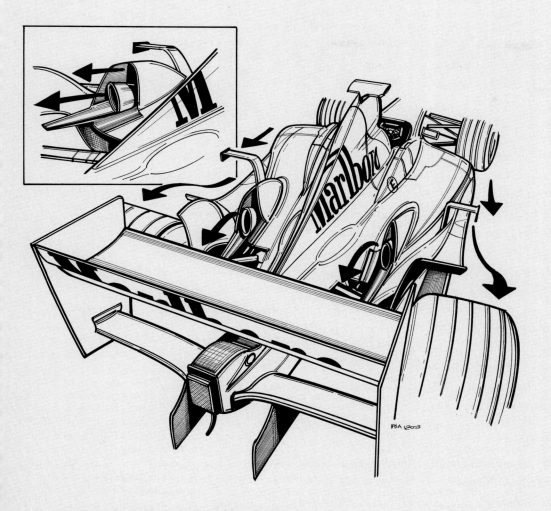

Introduced by Ferrari in 2002, the periscope exhaust ducts were further exasperated on the F2003 GA. Compared with last season's F2002, the 2003 Ferrari also had larger fairings that allowed the airflow over the rear wing to be speeded up. The particular shape of these elements also allowed hot air to be extracted from the engine bay, which helped to reduce the working temperature of the Italian V10 engine.

Another refined technical solution of the Ferrari was the totally faired 'basket' brakes (right). The closed inside of the wheel was accompanied by the fairing of the external part, thus improving aerodynamics and the cooling of the braking system.

In the design on the right, note the attention paid by Ferrari aerodynamicists to the flow of air over the rear. The lower part of the sides has been dug out and the sidepods present a clear tapering towards the bottom.

DESIGN: P. D'ALESSIO

WILLIAMS FW 25

Some cars are perfect right from the start (for example last year's Ferrari F2002), others reach perfection during the season: this was the case of the Williams-BMW FW25 which, after a difficult start, from the Monaco Grand Prix onwards became the car to beat and the best car in the 2003 world championship. Nevertheless shakedown tests had made Williams-BMW fear the worst. Contrary to pre-season forecasts and despite the optimistic declarations of Patrick Head and Gerhard Berger, once the FW25 took to the track it even failed to live up to the performances of last year's car. It was even thought that the FW25 would have to be redesigned or a 'B' version introduced and that the season was over before it had even begun! Proof of the scarce competitiveness of the first version of the 2003 Williams was the decision taken by the Grove-based team to start the season with a hybrid car. This was fitted with the old rear suspension while the new gearbox with its incorporated rear suspension was made competitive. The decision limited the potential of the Anglo-German car, but did not prevent Juan Pablo Montoya from coming close to victory in the spectacular Australian GP. The next few races however demonstrated the car's limits and apart from Ralf Schumacher's first few laps in the lead of the San Marino Grand Prix, the FW25's limits were plain for all to see and its drivers were never able to challenge for the top slots. Then suddenly, from the Monaco Grand Prix onwards, the Williams-BMW became the car to beat, thanks to Frank Dernie, a man of great experience and former engineer for the British team during the Mansell/Piquet period. According to Montoya, Dernie completely changed the car's set-up and this allowed the car's potential to emerge. This may be true but it is difficult to believe that one man could have overturned such a negative situation. It is more likely that Williams' resurrection was due to a complex series of factors. The first was clearly the technical ele-

DESIGN: P. D'ALESSIO

118

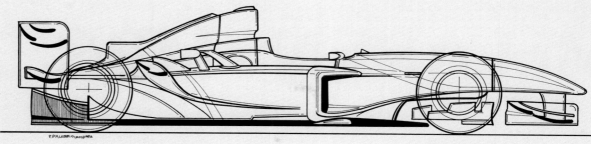

The view from above shows the car as it was at the start of the season (above) and mid-season (below). Compared with the versions used by Montoya and Schumacher in the early rounds of the championship, the evolution version sported 'chimney stack' bodywork for the disposal of hot air from the engine bay.

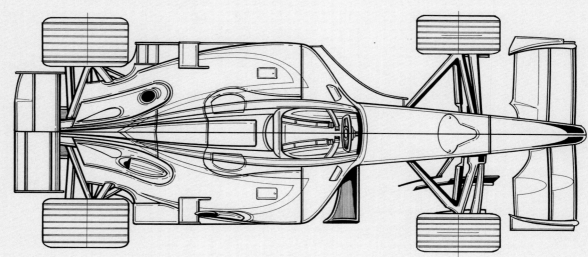

ment. The FW25, as previously mentioned, was a car with a constant growth potential: it was heavily modified at each race and its performance increased as a result.

Grove engineers were working in all directions: on the chassis, the suspension, but above all on the aerodynamics package, which saw the front and rear wings, bargeboards, rear diffusers and the shape of the chimney stacks altered over and over again. For their part, BMW engineers were concentrating efforts into beating Ferrari and above all their Mercedes 'cousins'. On the eve of the US GP, BMW issued an official press release, rather strangely for modern-day Formula 1, in which the characteristics of its V10 engine were revealed. The engine put out more than 900 BHP of power at 19200 rpm, a figure considered unimaginable until a few years ago, but it is reckoned that the figure is close to 950 BHP at 20000 rpm ... and all this encased in a metal box weighing 90 kilograms.

The most important element in the resurgence of the Anglo-German team was however the tyre factor and the progress made by Michelin after a disastrous 2002 was simply incredible. It was due to the brand-new compounds and the new tyre carcasses introduced in 2003, defined as revolutionary by Michelin boss Pierre Dupasquier. The new more rigid carcass adapted better than the Bridgestone tyres to the characteristics of this year's Williams, but some advantage was also gained from the controversial larger-profile front tyres that caused a major rumpus in Formula 1 before the Hungarian GP and led the FIA to intervene and force Michelin to make a U-turn.

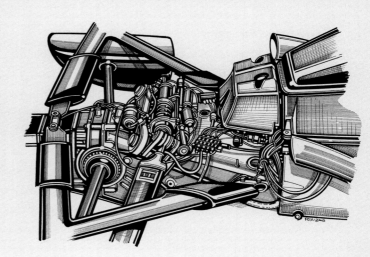

McLAREN MP4/17D

Until last year no team, not even those fighting for the title, would have considered starting the championship with the previous year's car. Then came Ferrari, which starting from 2002, led the way in this new trend. The first few races of the season were to be raced with the trusty and reliable old car, and then the new model would make its debut only when it had reached a competitive level. In 2003 McLaren boss Ron Dennis tried to go one better than his 'hated' Italian rivals: run the whole season with the old car, while the revolutionary MP4-18 was developed for the track. One of the most clamorous bluffs in the history of F1 was a 40 million dollar mistake...

Despite their double commitment (development of the MP4/17D and the creation of the MP4/18), McLaren had a superb season with a car that was much more competitive than last year's model. The letter 'D', which was added to the MP4/17, indicated the fourth evolution 'step' and the car was brand-new in many aspects albeit not a new model. Numerous improvements were made to Raikkonen and Coulthard's McLarens, starting with a radical aerodynamic facelift from Adrian Newey, with new front wings and a totally new rear wing with a Renault-type spoiler profile and new bargeboards, which were different for different circuits.

The 2003 car also had a different weight distribution and Mercedes made available for McLaren a heavily revised F0110M engine, even though paddock insiders maintain that there was still a 40-50 BHP difference in power between the Ferrari-BMW engines and the Mercedes. McLaren engineers also focussed on new front and rear suspension layouts. At the rear the MP4/17D had an evolution step suspension over last year's version, with a third transversal shock absorber and relative coaxial springing giving better control over pitch and roll. At the front, after the modifications of the start of the year, the MP4/18's suspension was transplanted onto the MP4/17D at the British Grand Prix. This layout improved the behaviour of the car and allowed the drivers to exploit better the characteristics of the Michelin radials, which were the real ace up the sleeve of Ferrari's rivals in 2003. As mentioned before however the MP4/17D must be considered as a stopgap car before the revolutionary, albeit mysterious MP4/18, which was only seen in private testing, appeared. There were numerous innovations in this expensive travelling laboratory; starting with the nose, which was 'ant-eater' style, very narrow at the front, moved back from the front wing and almost attached to it. The area between the front suspensions, with their low wishbone strut mountings,

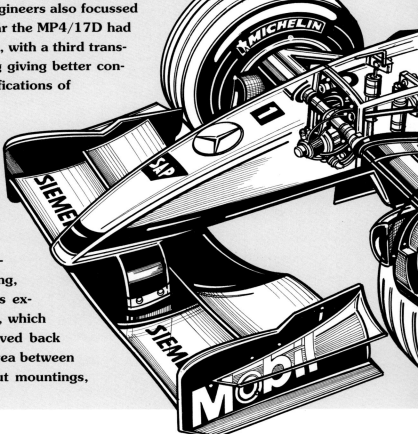

was similar to the MP4/17D. The MP4/18 did not however have large lateral boards, which were replaced by smaller deflectors, similar to Ferrari. The sides were also different and shorter than the MP4/17D, and the rear was characterised by being extremely tapered. From a mechanical point of view, the MP4/18 had a traditional gearbox, until the carbon-fibre transmission unit and a revised Mercedes V10 were introduced, but during numerous tests the latter failed to convince. The exhausts were also another unconvincing feature because after making its debut with low exhausts that exited directly into the rear diffuser, the MP4/18 had to resort to the more traditional high exhausts to avoid the danger of self-ignition in the lower rear diffuser and unpredictable behaviour in the car when exiting curves.

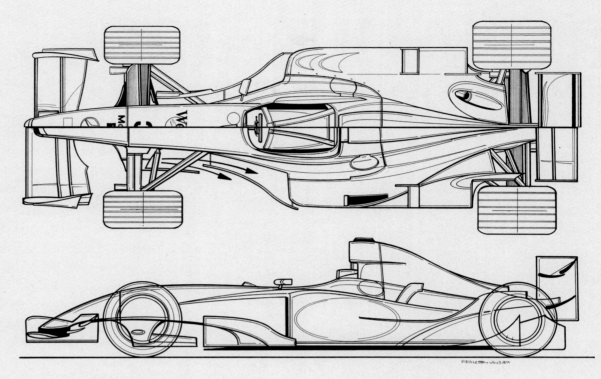

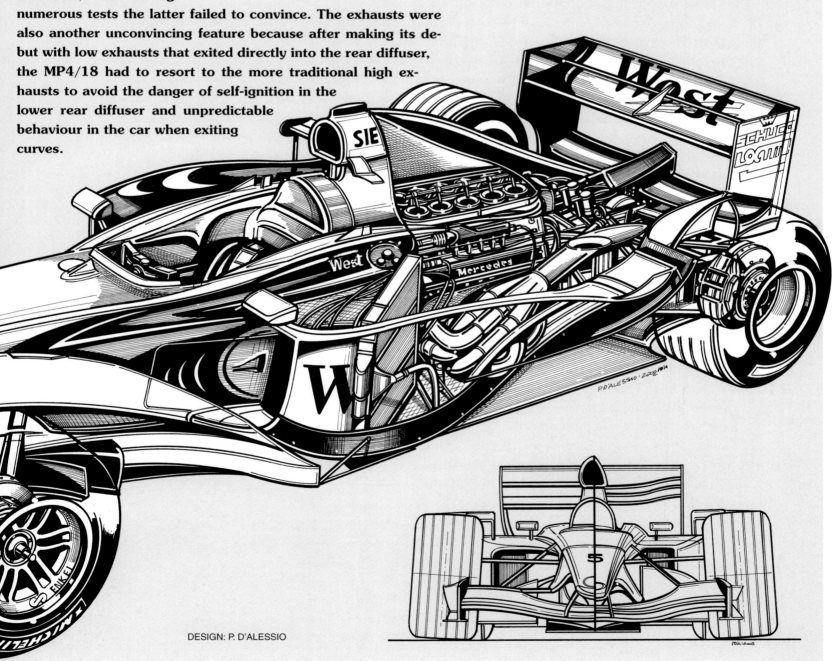

DESIGN: P. D'ALESSIO

RENAULT R23

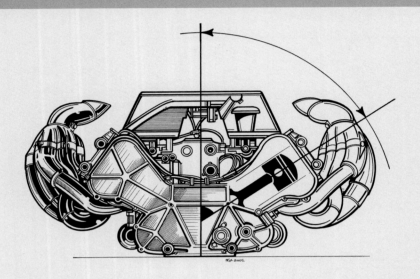

At the start of the 2003 championship few people would have gambled on Renault winning any races, but right from the early rounds the French team were right on the pace and battling with Ferrari, McLaren-Mercedes and Williams-BMW. What was the reason for this unexpected improvement? As always in these cases, the increase in performance was not the result of one change, but determined by a series of modifications made to the car over the winter. Even though the R23 was not that much different externally to the 2002 car, there was probably not one sector in which Renault designer, Mike Gascoigne had not made any significant changes. Let's start with the aerodynamics. In 2003 the Renault was converted to the 'comma-shaped' wing profiles, both at the front and the rear, and the car was able to increase downforce but with a minimal increase in wind resistance.

The sides were also different, with wide side deflectors just in front of the rear wheels. At the British Grand Prix, Renault debuted a new rear end, which was lower and more tapered than the previous one and new 'chimney stacks' to extract the hot air from the engine bay. In the R23 these extracted air at the same place as the small lateral flaps and improved efficiency. Those were all the changes regarding the appearance of the car, but under the skin of Trulli's and Alonso's Renaults there were a number of innovations, starting with the light composite materials chassis, which many observers reckoned was the best structure in 2003. Confirmation of the excellent work carried out in this sector by Mike Gascoyne came at circuits where real driving ability was required, with long curves, where the Renaults were unbeatable: tracks like the Hungaroring, where Fernando Alonso scored the first win of his career. The car's perfect balance was also the result of positive collaboration between Renault engineers and Michelin technicians, who developed the 2003 tyres in collaboration with Williams and McLaren but above all with Renault. It is no mystery that the Clermont-Ferrand based tyre manufacturer aims to win the world championship in the coming years with an all-French team, to crown their dreams of grandeur that vanished at the start of the 1980s when Alain Prost, Renault's #1 driver at the time, twice failed in his objective. They still have some way to go however because while the aerodynamics and the chassis of the R23 are superb, the same cannot be said of the French car's engine. Even though Renault complains of 100 BHP performance gap from the other top engines, it is clear that the French ten-cylinder engine does not have the same power output as the Ferrari, Mercedes or BMW units. This is the fault of the engine's architecture and the 111° Vee, which despite helping to lower the car's centre of gravity, prevents engine revs from being increased beyond a certain limit. To get round this problem, which has continued since 2001, Flavio Briatore's team has divorced from Jean-Jacques His, the engine designer, and in 2004 hopes to revert to a narrower Vee angle, probably 72°.

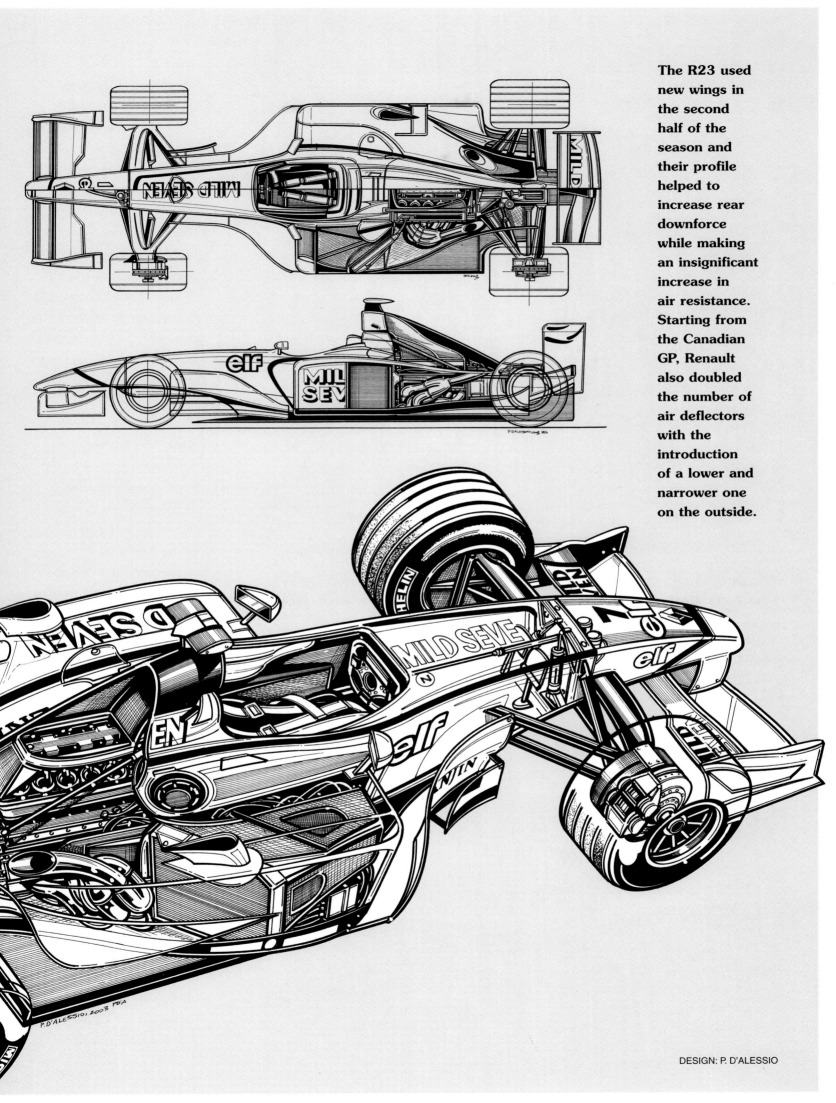

The R23 used new wings in the second half of the season and their profile helped to increase rear downforce while making an insignificant increase in air resistance. Starting from the Canadian GP, Renault also doubled the number of air deflectors with the introduction of a lower and narrower one on the outside.

DESIGN: P. D'ALESSIO

F.1 RENAULT STORY

There are many ways to reach success in Formula 1. Some teams get there after years and years of trying, others spend millions of dollars, others use existing competitive technical structures. Renault does not belong to any of these categories. Every time it enters F1 it does so by going against the grain and proposing something new, revolutionary even. That has been the case since 1977 when the first turbo engine in F1 history made its debut at Silverstone. It was the same in 1989, when the French manufacturer decided to return to F1 with a brand-new, ten-cylinder, normally aspirated 3.5 litre Vee engine. And it was the same in 2001 when Renault not only decided to build everything in-house, from the engine to the chassis. It took over Benetton and then did it in its own inimitable style by creating the most original and innovative car in recent years, with an unusual 111° V10 engine. In these pages we have a brief look at the most important chapters in Renault's F1 history from 1977 to the present day.

1977 RENAULT RS 01

For its debut in Formula 1, Renault opted for the most complex and difficult route: turbo power. The rules in force in 1977 stipulated that there had to be a 2:1 ration between normally-aspirated and turbocharged engines and therefore the cylinder size of the latter could not exceed 1500 cc. Despite this, in 1978, its first season in Formula 1, the RS/01 (this page) scored points and in the 1979 South African Grand Prix Jean-Pierre Jabouille started from pole position. Alongside, the Renault V6 turbo engine.

1979 RENAULT RS 10

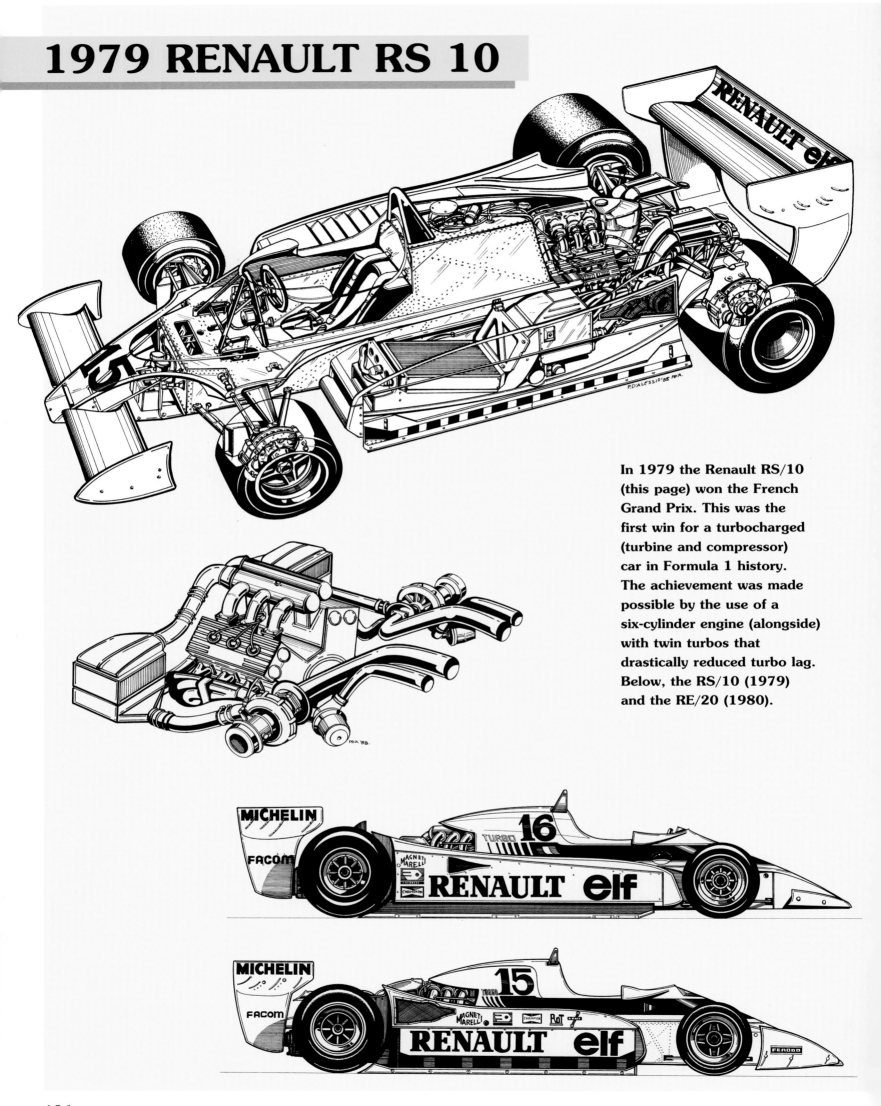

In 1979 the Renault RS/10 (this page) won the French Grand Prix. This was the first win for a turbocharged (turbine and compressor) car in Formula 1 history. The achievement was made possible by the use of a six-cylinder engine (alongside) with twin turbos that drastically reduced turbo lag. Below, the RS/10 (1979) and the RE/20 (1980).

1985 LOTUS-RENAULT

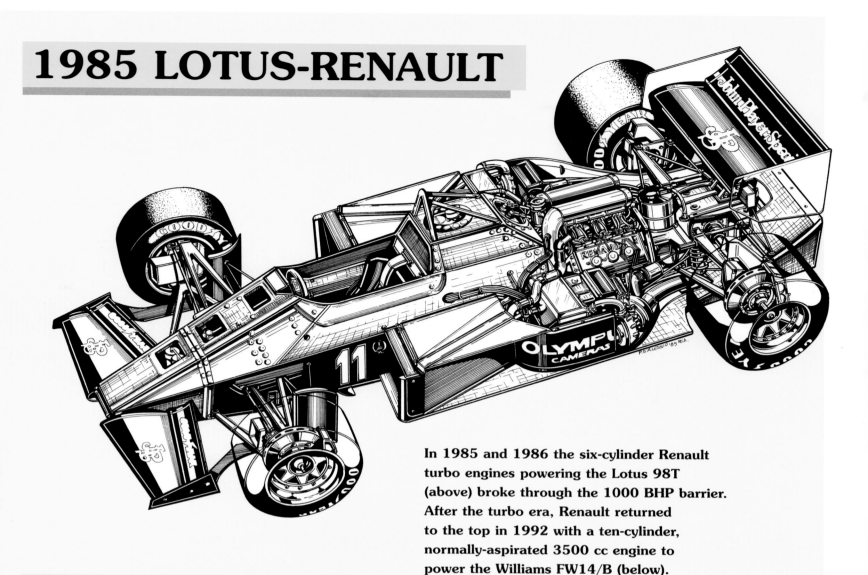

In 1985 and 1986 the six-cylinder Renault turbo engines powering the Lotus 98T (above) broke through the 1000 BHP barrier. After the turbo era, Renault returned to the top in 1992 with a ten-cylinder, normally-aspirated 3500 cc engine to power the Williams FW14/B (below). Nigel Mansell dominated the season, followed by Alain Prost in 1993 and Damon Hill/Jacques Villeneuve in 1996 and 1997.

1992 WILLIAMS

PHOTOCOLOR: P. D'ALESSIO

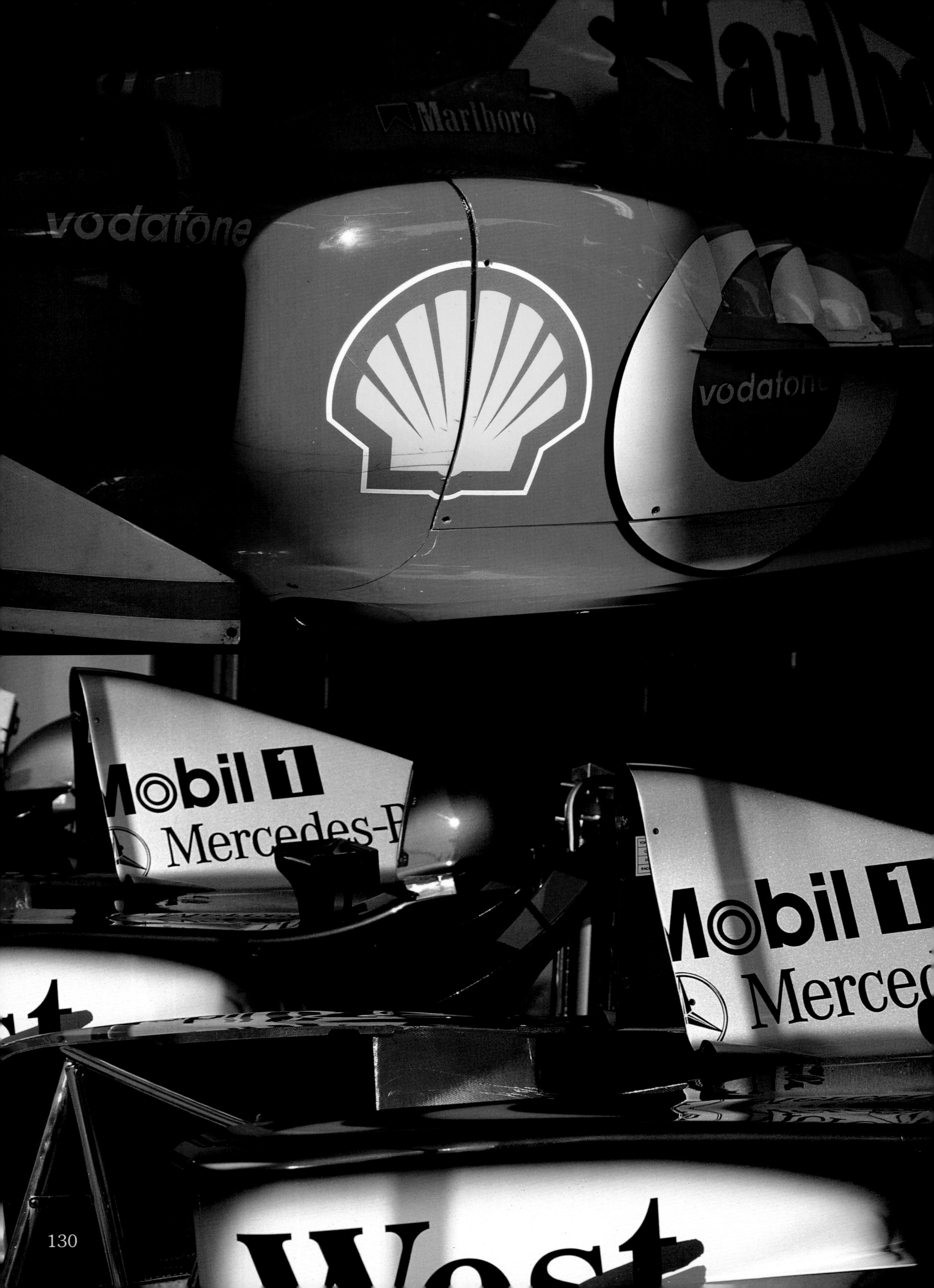
Marlboro
vodafone
vodafone
Mobil 1
Mobil 1
West

PHOTOCOLOR: P. D'ALESSIO

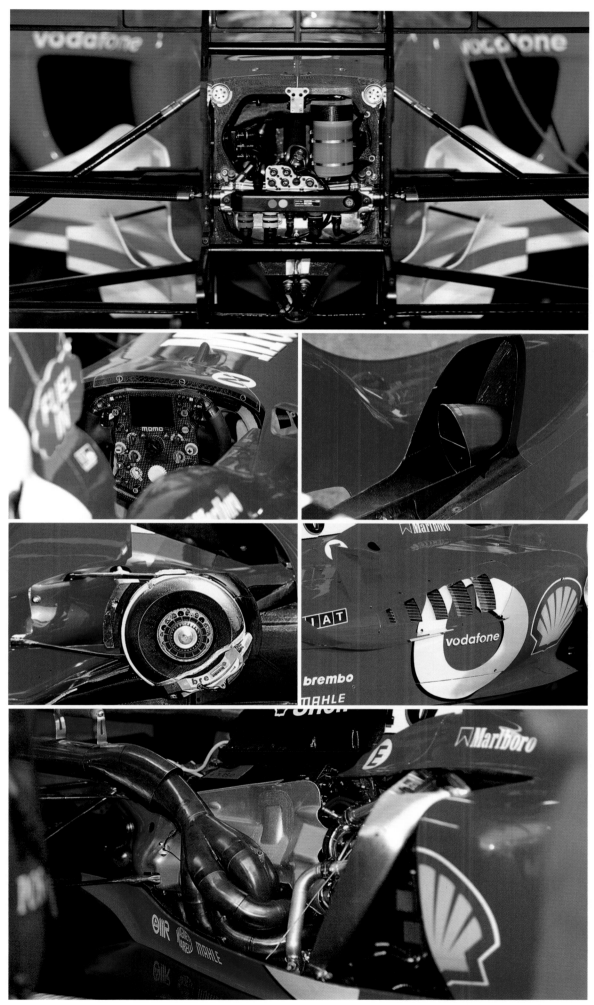

PHOTOCOLORS: P. D'ALESSIO

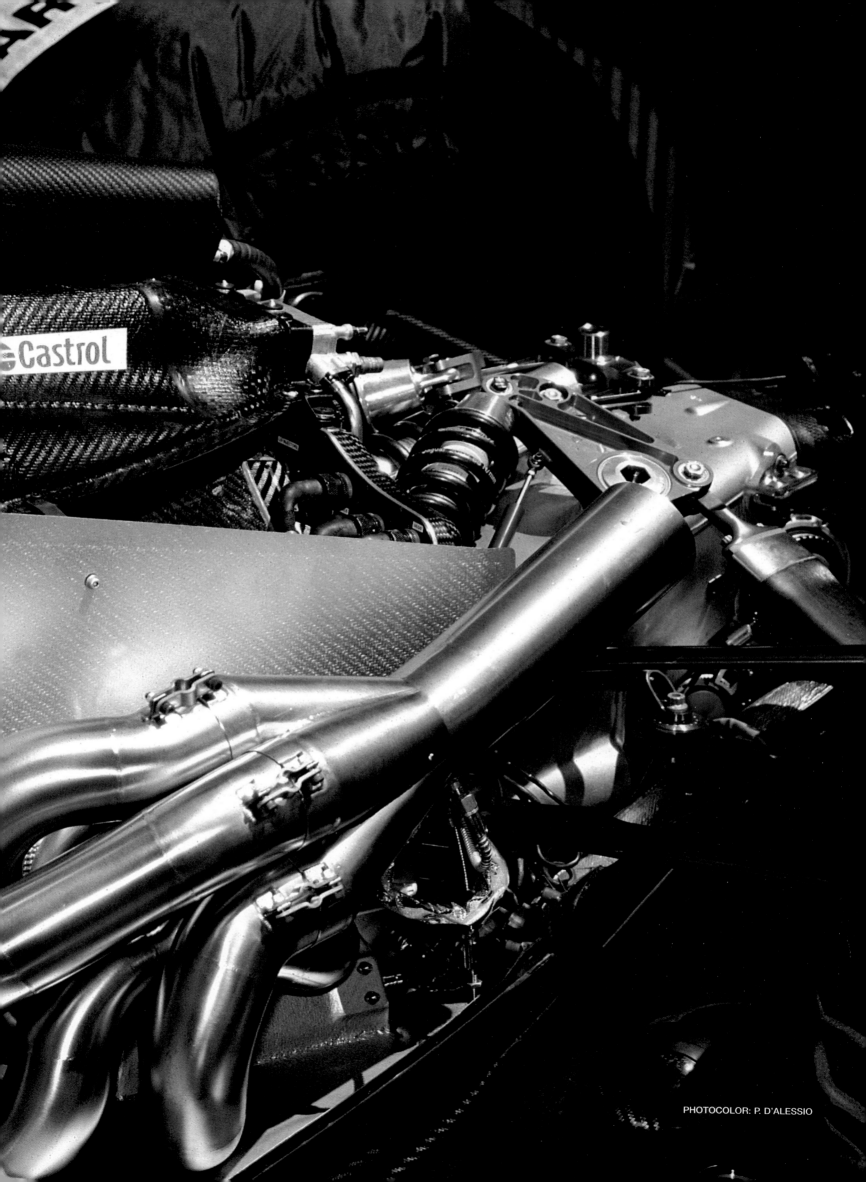

Castrol

PHOTOCOLOR: P. D'ALESSIO

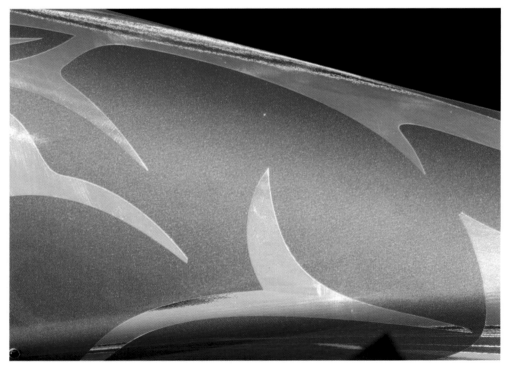

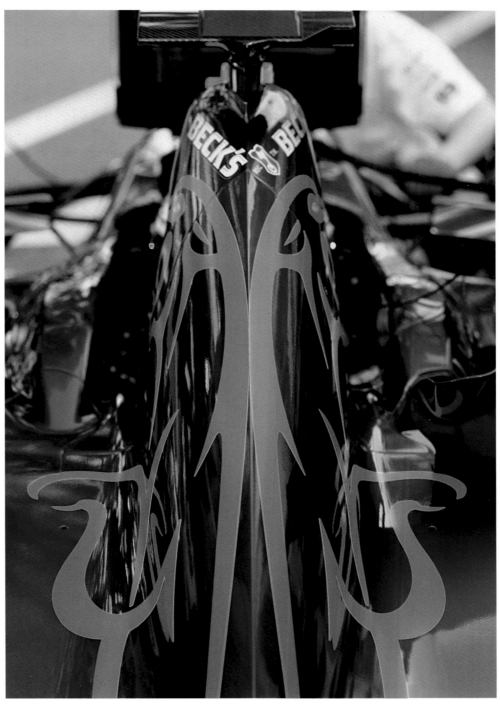

PHOTOCOLORS: P. D'ALESSIO

PHOTOCOLOR: P. D'ALESSIO

 PHOTOCOLORS: P. D'ALESSIO

PHOTOCOLORS: P. D'ALESSIO

F1 2003

POLE POSITION

2003 MICHAEL SCHUMACHER

2 **1** **3**

1°	2°	3°

STARTING GRID

MICHAEL SCHUMACHER
FERRARI
1'27"173

JUAN PABLO MONTOYA
WILLIAMS
1'28"101

OLIVIER PANIS
TOYOTA
1'28"288

NICK HEIDFELD
SAUBER
1'28"464

RALF SCHUMACHER
WILLIAMS
1'28"830

DAVID COULTHARD
McLAREN
1'29"105

GIANCARLO FISICHELLA
JORDAN
1'29"344

KIMI RAIKKONEN
McLAREN
1'29"470

RALPH FIRMAN
JORDAN
1'31"242

JOS VERSTAPPEN
MINARDI

RUBENS BARRICHELLO
FERRARI
1'27"418

H.HARALD FRENTZEN
SAUBER
1'28"274

JACQUES VILLENEUVE
BAR
1'28"420

JENSON BUTTON
BAR
1'28"682

FERNANDO ALONSO
RENAULT
1'28"928

JARNO TRULLI
RENAULT
1'29"136

MARK WEBBER
JAGUAR
1'29"367

CRISTIANO DA MATTA
TOYOTA
1'29"538

ANTONIO PIZZONIA
JAGUAR
1'31"723

JUSTIN WILSON
MINARDI

RESULTS

	DRIVER	CAR	KPH	GAP
1	D. Coulthard	McLaren	194,868	-
2	J.P. Montoya	Williams	194,571	8"675
3	K. Raikkonen	McLaren	194,553	9"192
4	M. Schumacher	Ferrari	194,543	9"482
5	J. Trulli	Renault	193,546	38"801
6	H.H. Frentzen	Sauber	193,373	43"928
7	F. Alonso	Renault	193,334	45"074
8	R. Schumacher	Williams	193,312	45"745
9	J. Villeneuve	BAR	192,646	1'05"536
10	J. Button	BAR	192,631	1'05"974
11	J. Verstappen	Minardi	188,473	1 lap
12	G. Fisichella	Jordan	190,863	6 laps
13	A. Pizzonia	Jaguar	189,664	6 laps

RETIREMENTS

O. Panis	Toyota	31	Fuel pressure
N. Heidfeld	Sauber	20	Suspension
J. Wilson	Minardi	16	Engine
M. Webber	Jaguar	15	Suspension
C. Da Matta	Toyota	7	Crashed
R. Firman	Jordan	6	Crashed
R. Barrichello	Ferrari	5	Crashed

THE RACE

DRIVER	LAP	FASTEST LAP	AVERAGE SPEED (KPH)	TOP SPEED
K. Raikkonen	32	1'27"724	217,623	316,400
M. Schumacher	27	1'27"759	217,536	318,400
J.P. Montoya	39	1'27"942	217,083	311,200
F. Alonso	35	1'28"170	216,522	313,500
D. Coulthard	28	1'28"272	216,272	314,800
J. Button	57	1'28"600	215,471	312,600
R. Schumacher	37	1'28"617	215,430	314,400
J. Trulli	44	1'28"638	215,379	309,100
J. Villeneuve	57	1'28"770	215,059	312,100
H.H. Frentzen	35	1'29"096	214,272	310,300
A. Pizzonia	37	1'29"217	213,981	308,900
G. Fisichella	49	1'29"274	213,845	309,100
O. Panis	23	1'29"694	212,843	310,700
M. Webber	14	1'29"697	212,836	313,400
J. Verstappen	29	1'31"785	207,994	301,700
J. Wilson	13	1'33"139	204,971	303,900
N. Heidfeld	14	1'33"519	204,138	309,900
C. Da Matta	7	1'33"753	203,628	309,800
R. Firman	6	1'36"644	197,537	304,800
R. Barrichello	5	1'37"086	196,638	304,900

Australian GP

THE CIRCUIT

9 March 2003
Circuit: Melbourne
Km.: 5,303
Laps: 58
Distance: 307,574 Kms

Michelin Triumph

The Formula 1 season kicked off as always in Australia, but this time with new regulations. Friday qualifying and Saturday's one-lap dash for pole again confirmed Ferrari superiority with what was essentially a modified 2002 car and Schumacher and Barrichello took the first two places on the starting-grid. The race was a real scorcher because half the field were on dry tyres and half on wets. Only Raikkonen decided to return to the pits after the warm-up lap and the Finn had to start from the pit-lane on slick tyres.

This proved to be the right choice because on lap 17 the young Finnish driver was already in the lead and only a drive-through penalty imposed for speeding in the pit-lane prevented him from taking the win.

Meanwhile the Ferraris were suffering badly. Barrichello, possibly disturbed by a radio call, crashed heavily at Turn Five and was out of the race. Michael did what he could as the track dried out but was not the dominant force he had been throughout last season and two-thirds into the race the German went onto the gravel and damaged his bargeboards.

For a couple of laps one of the two side deflectors remained stuck under the car before eventually falling off. Montoya was now in the lead and heading for the second win of his career, but ten laps from the end amazingly ran wide at the famous Turn One. This handed the lead to Coulthard, who so far had hardly figured in the race, but the Scot held on until the chequered flag. Montoya was second and Raikkonen third after being forced to come in for a drive-through penalty.

A superb Australian GP had been conditioned by the weather, by two appearances of the safety car in the space of a few laps, but above all by Schumacher being forced to play catch-up.

HIGHLIGHTS

Michelin scored a 1-2-3 podium finish for the first time since returning to Formula 1 in 2001. The French manufacturer's first-ever win in Formula 1 dates back to 1978 when Reutemann won the Brazilian Grand Prix in a Ferrari, while their first world title came the following year when Jody Scheckter won for Ferrari. Michelin retired from Formula 1 in 1984 after winning the championship with Niki Lauda and McLaren. They finally returned to Formula 1 in 2001.

PHOTO PORTFOLIO
PREVIOUS PAGES

Parc fermé is one of the innovations in the 2003 championship. For the mechanics, gone are the days of long sleepless nights spent getting the cars ready for the following day, except on rare occasions.
In the last photo, Montoya's mistake just a few laps from the end which cost him almost certain victory.

CHAMPIONSHIP POINTS		AUSTRALIAN GP	MALAYSIAN GP	BRAZILIAN GP	SAN MARINO GP	SPANISH GP	AUSTRIAN GP	MONACO GP	CANADIAN GP	EUROPEAN GP	FRENCH GP	BRITISH GP	GERMAN GP	HUNGARIAN GP	ITALIAN GP	UNITED STATES GP	JAPANESE GP	TOTAL POINTS
1	D. Coulthard	10																10
2	J.P. Montoya	8																8
3	K. Raikkonen	6																6
4	M. Schumacher	5																5
5	J. Trulli	4																4
6	H.H. Frentzen	3																3
7	F. Alonso	2																2
8	R. Schumacher	1																1
9	R. Barrichello	-																0
10	M. Webber	-																0
11	A. Pizzonia	-																0
12	N. Heidfeld	-																0
13	J. Villeneuve	-																0
14	J. Button	-																0
15	G. Fisichella	-																0
16	R. Firman	-																0
17	J. Verstappen	-																0
18	J. Wilson	-																0
19	O. Panis	-																0
20	C. Da Matta	-																0

POLE POSITION

2003 FERNANDO ALONSO

'90	-
'91	-
'92	-
'93	-
'94	-
'95	-
'96	-
'97	-
'98	-
'99	M. Schumacher
'00	M. Schumacher
'01	M. Schumacher
'02	M. Schumacher

2 1 3

	1°	2°	3°
'90	-	-	-
'91	-	-	-
'92	-	-	-
'93	-	-	-
'94	-	-	-
'95	-	-	-
'96	-	-	-
'97	-	-	-
'98	-	-	-
'99	M. Hakkinen	M. Schumacher	E. Irvine
'00	M. Schumacher	D. Coulthard	R. Barrichello
'01	M. Schumacher	R. Barrichello	D. Coulthard
'02	R. Schumacher	J.P. Montoya	M. Schumacher

STARTING GRID

FERNANDO ALONSO
RENAULT
1'37"044

JARNO TRULLI
RENAULT
1'37"217

MICHAEL SCHUMACHER
FERRARI
1'37"393

DAVID COULTHARD
McLAREN
1'37"454

RUBENS BARRICHELLO
FERRARI
1'37"579

NICK HEIDFELD
SAUBER
1'37"766

KIMI RAIKKONEN
McLAREN
1'37"858

JUAN PABLO MONTOYA
WILLIAMS
1'37"974

JENSON BUTTON
BAR
1'38"073

OLIVIER PANIS
TOYOTA
1'38"094

CRISTIANO DA MATTA
TOYOTA
1'38"097

JACQUES VILLENEUVE
BAR
1'38"289

H.HARALD FRENTZEN
SAUBER
1'38"291

GIANCARLO FISICHELLA
JORDAN
1'38"416

ANTONIO PIZZONIA
JAGUAR
1'38"516

MARK WEBBER
JAGUAR
1'38"624

RALF SCHUMACHER
WILLIAMS
1'38"789

JOS VERSTAPPEN
MINARDI
1'40"417

JUSTIN WILSON
MINARDI
1'40"599

RALPH FIRMAN
JORDAN
1'40"910

RESULTS

	DRIVER	CAR	KPH	GAP
1	K. Raikkonen	McLaren	201,629	-
2	R. Barrichello	Ferrari	200,210	39"286
3	F. Alonso	Renault	199,327	1'04"007
4	R. Schumacher	Williams	198,476	1'28"026
5	J. Trulli	Renault	197,918	1 lap
6	M. Schumacher	Ferrari	197,804	1 lap
7	J. Button	BAR	197,797	1 lap
8	N. Heidfeld	Sauber	196,888	1 lap
9	H.H. Frentzen	Sauber	194,926	1 lap
10	R. Firman	Jordan	194,880	1 lap
11	C. Da Matta	Toyota	194,871	1 lap
12	J.P. Montoya	Williams	190,234	3 laps
13	J. Verstappen	Minardi	185,995	4 laps

RETIREMENTS

A. Pizzonia	Jaguar	42	Brakes
J. Wilson	Minardi	41	Cramp
M. Webber	Jaguar	35	Engine
O. Panis	Toyota	12	Fuel pressure
D. Coulthard	McLaren	2	Electrical fault
J. Villeneuve	BAR	0	Gearbox
G. Fisichella	Jordan	0	Clutch

THE RACE

DRIVER	LAP	FASTEST LAP	AVERAGE SPEED (KPH)	TOP SPEED
M. Schumacher	45	1'36"412	206,974	311,500
R. Barrichello	24	1'36"542	206,695	311,800
K. Raikkonen	10	1'36"764	206,221	309,900
F. Alonso	12	1'37"078	205,554	306,400
J. Trulli	53	1'37"484	204,698	305,500
J.P. Montoya	26	1'37"787	204,063	317,200
D. Coulthard	2	1'38"021	203,576	298,600
R. Schumacher	24	1'38"071	203,472	302,700
C. Da Matta	35	1'38"156	203,296	310,500
O. Panis	7	1'38"176	203,255	308,700
J. Button	10	1'38"413	202,765	306,200
M. Webber	6	1'38"464	202,660	304,500
N. Heidfeld	9	1'38"528	202,529	303,200
A. Pizzonia	3	1'38"572	202,438	301,900
H.H. Frentzen	19	1'39"287	200,980	307,200
R. Firman	14	1'39"665	200,218	304,100
J. Verstappen	3	1'39"667	200,214	303,700
J. Wilson	12	1'39"752	200,044	305,000
J. Villeneuve	-	-	-	-
G. Fisichella	-	-	-	-

Malaysian GP

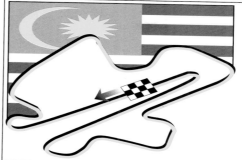

THE CIRCUIT

23 March 2003
Circuit: Sepang
Km.: 5,543
Laps: 56
Distance: 310,408 Kms

Rookie Triumph

The start of the 2003 season is throwing up a series of surprises. First Ferrari losing in Australia, then Malaysia with the all-Renault front row and the first pole position for talented youngster Alonso. Finally a surprise podium at Sepang with Raikkonen and Alonso sandwiching 'veteran' Barrichello in second place, saving Ferrari's honour.

In qualifying the surprise came, as mentioned, from Renault, which locked in the front row with Alonso and Trulli thanks to an extraordinary performance by the Michelin tyres in the heat and a superb-handling chassis, which made up for less horsepower and a top speed that was considerably inferior than the opposition.

At the start Alonso got the 'holeshot' to lead into the first corner, while Trulli, Coulthard and Schumacher were battling behind. The German then hit the rear tyre of Trulli's Renault, ruining his nosecone and earning himself a drive-through penalty.

At this point the battle was between Alonso and Raikkonen, who switched places during the pit-stop action. Ten laps from the end, Raikkonen came in for his second and final pit-stop and when he returned to the track the Finn had a twenty second lead over Barrichello, followed by Alonso. His team told him to control the race and the young Finn did so with ice-cool ease.

The positions remained the same until the chequered flag, with Ralf Schumacher finishing fourth, Trulli fifth and Michael Schumacher sixth. After the race the Renault team had harsh words to say about Schumacher for his risky move on Trulli, which probably deprived the Italian of a well-deserved podium finish.

But it was also a sign of nervousness for the five-times world champion, who is probably no longer used to seeing so many cars driven by rookies ahead of him.

HIGHLIGHTS

The 22 year-old Spanish driver from Oviedo, Fernando Alonso, set the first pole position of his career at Sepang and followed this up with his first podium. Alonso made his F1 debut in 2001 with Minardi and put in some sterling drives in his first season despite not scoring any points. At 24 years of age, Kimi Raikkonen scored his first win in F1. The Finn also made his debut in 2001 with Sauber, switching to McLaren-Mercedes the following year when he obtained four podiums (1 second place and 3 thirds).

PHOTO PORTFOLIO
PREVIOUS PAGES

Trulli and Schumacher make contact shortly after the start. That was the end of the Italian's chances of obtaining a good result after qualifying on the front row of the grid, together with team-mate Alonso.
On the podium, two F1 youngsters: Raikkonen takes his first win and Alonso his first podium.

	CHAMPIONSHIP POINTS	AUSTRALIAN GP	MALAYSIAN GP	BRAZILIAN GP	SAN MARINO GP	SPANISH GP	AUSTRIAN GP	MONACO GP	CANADIAN GP	EUROPEAN GP	FRENCH GP	BRITISH GP	GERMAN GP	HUNGARIAN GP	ITALIAN GP	UNITED STATES GP	JAPANESE GP	TOTAL POINTS
1	K. Raikkonen	6	10															16
2	D. Coulthard	10	-															10
3	J.P. Montoya	8	-															8
4	R. Barrichello	-	8															8
5	F. Alonso	2	6															8
6	M. Schumacher	5	3															8
7	J. Trulli	4	4															8
8	R. Schumacher	1	5															6
9	H.H. Frentzen	3	-															3
10	J. Button	-	2															2
11	N. Heidfeld	-	1															1
12	M. Webber	-	-															0
13	A. Pizzonia	-	-															0
14	J. Villeneuve	-	-															0
15	G. Fisichella	-	-															0
16	R. Firman	-	-															0
17	J. Verstappen	-	-															0
18	J. Wilson	-	-															0
19	O. Panis	-	-															0
20	C. Da Matta	-	-															0

POLE POSITION

2003 RUBENS BARRICHELLO

'90	A. Senna
'91	A. Senna
'92	N. Mansell
'93	A. Prost
'94	A. Senna
'95	D. Hill
'96	D. Hill
'97	J. Villeneuve
'98	M. Hakkinen
'99	M. Hakkinen
'00	M. Hakkinen
'01	M. Schumacher
'02	J.P. Montoya

2 **1** **3**

	1°	2°	3°
'90	A. Prost	G. Berger	A. Senna
'91	A. Senna	R. Patrese	G. Berger
'92	N. Mansell	R. Patrese	M. Schumacher
'93	A. Senna	D. Hill	M. Schumacher
'94	M. Schumacher	D. Hill	J. Alesi
'95	G. Berger	M. Hakkinen	J. Alesi
'96	D. Hill	J. Alesi	M. Schumacher
'97	J. Villeneuve	G. Berger	O. Panis
'98	M. Hakkinen	D. Coulthard	M. Schumacher
'99	M. Hakkinen	M. Schumacher	H.H. Frentzen
'00	M. Schumacher	G. Fisichella	H.H. Frentzen
'01	D. Coulthard	M. Schumacher	N. Heidfeld
'02	M. Schumacher	R. Schumacher	D. Coulthard

STARTING GRID

RUBENS BARRICHELLO
FERRARI
1'13"807

MARK WEBBER
JAGUAR
1'13"851

JARNO TRULLI
RENAULT
1'13"953

MICHAEL SCHUMACHER
FERRARI
1'14"130

JUAN PABLO MONTOYA
WILLIAMS
1'14"223

JENSON BUTTON
BAR
1'14"504

JACQUES VILLENEUVE
BAR
1'14"668

OLIVIER PANIS
TOYOTA
1'14"839

ANTONIO PIZZONIA
JAGUAR
1'15"317

JOS VERSTAPPEN
MINARDI
1'16"542

DAVID COULTHARD
MCLAREN
1'13"818

KIMI RAIKKONEN
MCLAREN
1'13"866

RALF SCHUMACHER
WILLIAMS
1'14"124

GIANCARLO FISICHELLA
JORDAN
1'14"191

FERNANDO ALONSO
RENAULT
1'14"384

NICK HEIDFELD
SAUBER
1'14"631

H.HARALD FRENTZEN
SAUBER
1'14"839

RALPH FIRMAN
JORDAN
1'15"240

CRISTIANO DA MATTA
TOYOTA
1'15"641

JUSTIN WILSON
MINARDI
1'15"586

RESULTS

	DRIVER	CAR	KPH	GAP
1	K. Raikkonen	McLaren	152,423	-
2	G. Fisichella	Jordan	152,400	0"831
3	F. Alonso	Renault	152,234	6"695
4	D. Coulthard	McLaren	152,215	7"391
5	H.H. Frentzen	Sauber	152,158	9"392
6	J. Villeneuve	BAR	151,919	17"910
7	M. Webber	Jaguar	151,858	20"070
8	J. Trulli	Renault	151,760	23"569
9	R. Schumacher	Williams	151,481	33"556
10	C. Da Matta	Toyota	148,743	1 lap

RETIREMENTS

R. Barrichello	Ferrari	46	Fuel pressure
J. Button	BAR	32	Crashed
J. Verstappen	Minardi	30	Spun off
M. Schumacher	Ferrari	26	Crashed
J.P. Montoya	Williams	24	Crashed
A. Pizzonia	Jaguar	24	Crashed
O. Panis	Toyota	17	Accident
R. Firman	Jordan	17	Accident
J. Wilson	Minardi	15	Spun off
N. Heidfeld	Sauber	8	Engine

THE RACE

DRIVER	LAP	FASTEST LAP	AVERAGE SPEED (KPH)	TOP SPEED
R. Barrichello	46	1'22"032	189,101	276,900
H.H. Frentzen	53	1'23"089	186,696	267,800
D. Coulthard	40	1'23"132	186,599	289,000
G. Fisichella	51	1'23"454	185,879	266,700
F. Alonso	41	1'23"770	185,178	275,400
M. Schumacher	18	1'24"040	184,583	275,500
K. Raikkonen	39	1'24"104	184,443	267,500
J. Villeneuve	48	1'24"463	183,659	286,700
R. Schumacher	46	1'24"778	182,976	289,600
M. Webber	50	1'24"956	182,593	277,800
J. Trulli	43	1'25"036	182,421	284,900
J.P. Montoya	24	1'25"814	180,767	262,300
J. Button	17	1'26"042	180,288	249,600
C. Da Matta	47	1'27"080	178,139	264,700
A. Pizzonia	24	1'27"990	176,297	262,100
J. Verstappen	25	1'28"010	176,257	250,100
J. Wilson	15	1'28"023	176,231	240,700
R. Firman	13	1'29"159	173,985	251,900
O. Panis	17	1'30"494	171,419	236,500
N. Heidfeld	4	2'11"396	118,058	188,200

Brazilian GP

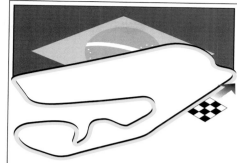

THE CIRCUIT

6 April 2003
Circuit: Interlagos
Km.: 4,309
Laps: 71
Distance: 305,909 Kms

Fisichella's finest hour!

Mark Webber, Kimi Raikkonen, Fernando Alonso and above all Giancarlo Fisichella all had their moment of glory in Brazil after the world's press had predicted a Schumacher walkover.
In qualifying, pole position went to Barrichello but the real surprise came from Mark Webber who clocked a fantastic third quickest time with the Jaguar, making up the second row of the grid alongside Raikkonen in his McLaren.
On Sunday the race got underway in a tropical downpour and the safety-car led the field for eight laps in an attempt to clear all the water from the track.
Barrichello was not entirely at ease in the wet and was overtaken by Coulthard and then by Raikkonen and Montoya, who powered past the Scot into the lead.
The race was an exciting one. The front suspension on Firman's Jordan failed and he crashed into Panis's Toyota. The safety car came out once again as the debris was cleared from the track.
A few laps later and the race was on but once again it was carnage. Between laps 25 and 32 all hell broke loose at Turn 3 which had a constant river of water running across. First Montoya slid off in the pool of water and crashed into the barriers, then a few seconds later Pizzonia did the same and crashed into the parked Williams, followed by Schumacher in his

Ferrari. The safety car came out for the third time but the problem still remained and Verstappen (Minardi) and Button (BAR) both went off the track at the same point.
Coulthard powered into the lead as the safety car dropped out, followed by Barrichello who took him a few laps later but the Brazilian's hopes for a victory at his home track were soon dashed as Barrichello ran out of fuel on lap 47. Coulthard stopped for a pit stop and Raikkonen and Fisichella moved into first and second place. The Italian scented the possibility of victory and attacked Raikkonen, overtaking him on lap 53. But one lap later Webber lost control at the final corner and crashed into the outside start-line track wall, sending a wheel and debris all over the track. Alonso crashed into the debris at full speed, destroying his Renault.
The Spanish driver stepped out of his car but was taken to hospital for a precautionary check-up.
The race was interrupted with Fisichella in the lead, but according to the regulations the standings were at the end of the previous lap and as a result the win went to Raikkonen, with Alonso third.
That was the way it stood for a few days because further checks revealed that the drivers had completed 56 laps, not 55 and at the end of lap 55 the leader was … Fisichella.

HIGHLIGHTS

Thirty-year-old Giancarlo Fisichella, with 110 grands prix to his name, took the first Formula 1 win of his career with the Jordan after the incident-packed race had been interrupted on lap 56.
Fisichella was another driver to make his Formula 1 debut with talent-scout team Minardi, in the 1996 Australian Grand Prix. He scored his first podium finish in the 1997 Canadian Grand Prix with Jordan-Peugeot.

PHOTO PORTFOLIO
PREVIOUS PAGES

The photos tell the story. The cars appear to have a mind of their own in the Sao Paulo downpour; Schumacher hits the wall, as do Alonso, Montoya, Pizzonia, Verstappen, Button, Firman and Panis.
To add to the chaos, Raikkonen was first proclaimed the winner, but the result was overturned and Fisichella eventually took his first GP victory.

	CHAMPIONSHIP POINTS	AUSTRALIAN GP	MALAYSIAN GP	BRAZILIAN GP	SAN MARINO GP	SPANISH GP	AUSTRIAN GP	MONACO GP	CANADIAN GP	EUROPEAN GP	FRENCH GP	BRITISH GP	GERMAN GP	HUNGARIAN GP	ITALIAN GP	UNITED STATES GP	JAPANESE GP	TOTAL POINTS
1	K. Raikkonen	6	10	**10**														26
2	D. Coulthard	10	-	5														15
3	F. Alonso	2	6	6														14
4	J. Trulli	4	4	1														9
5	J.P. Montoya	8	-	-														8
6	G. Fisichella	-	-	**8**														8
7	R. Barrichello	-	8	-														8
8	M. Schumacher	5	3	-														8
9	H.H. Frentzen	3	-	4														7
10	R. Schumacher	1	5	-														6
11	J. Villeneuve	-	-	3														3
12	J. Button	-	2	-														2
13	M. Webber	-	-	2														2
11	N. Heidfeld	-	1	-														1
13	A. Pizzonia	-	-	-														0
16	R. Firman	-	-	-														0
17	J. Verstappen	-	-	-														0
18	J. Wilson	-	-	-														0
19	O. Panis	-	-	-														0
20	C. Da Matta	-	-	-														0

POLE POSITION

2003
MICHAEL SCHUMACHER

'90	A. Senna
'91	A. Senna
'92	N. Mansell
'93	A. Prost
'94	A. Senna
'95	M. Schumacher
'96	M. Schumacher
'97	J. Villeneuve
'98	D. Coulthard
'99	M. Hakkinen
'00	M. Hakkinen
'01	D. Coulthard
'02	M. Schumacher

2 **1** **3**

	1°	2°	3°
'90	R. Patrese	G. Berger	A. Nannini
'91	A. Senna	G. Berger	J. Lehto
'92	N. Mansell	R. Patrese	A. Senna
'93	A. Prost	M. Schumacher	M. Brundle
'94	M. Schumacher	N. Larini	M. Hakkinen
'95	D. Hill	J. Alesi	G. Berger
'96	D. Hill	M. Schumacher	G. Berger
'97	H.H. Frentzen	M. Schumacher	E. irvine
'98	D. Coulthard	M. Schumacher	E. Irvine
'99	M. Schumacher	D. Coulthard	R. Barrichello
'00	M. Schumacher	M. Hakkinen	D. Coulthard
'01	R. Schumacher	D. Coulthard	R. Barichello
'02	M. Schumacher	R. Barrichello	R. Schumacher

STARTING GRID

MICHAEL SCHUMACHER
FERRARI
1'22"327

RUBENS BARRICHELLO
FERRARI
1'22"557

MARK WEBBER
JAGUAR
1'23"015

JACQUES VILLENEUVE
BAR
1'23"160

JENSON BUTTON
BAR
1'23"381

NICK HEIDFELD
SAUBER
1'23"700

CRISTIANO DA MATTA
TOYOTA
1'23"838

ANTONIO PIZZONIA
JAGUAR
1'24"147

GIANCARLO FISICHELLA
JORDAN
1'24"317

RALPH FIRMAN
JORDAN
1'26"357

RALF SCHUMACHER
WILLIAMS
1'22"341

JUAN PABLO MONTOYA
WILLIAMS
1'22"789

KIMI RAIKKONEN
MCLAREN
1'23"148

FERNANDO ALONSO
RENAULT
1'23"169

OLIVIER PANIS
TOYOTA
1'23"460

DAVID COULTHARD
MCLAREN
1'23"818

H.HARALD FRENTZEN
SAUBER
1'23"932

JARNO TRULLI
RENAULT
1'24"190

JUSTIN WILSON
MINARDI
1'25"826

JOS VERSTAPPEN
MINARDI

RESULTS

	DRIVER	CAR	KPH	GAP
1	M. Schumacher	Ferrari	207,894	-
2	K. Raikkonen	McLaren	207,821	1"882
3	R. Barrichello	Ferrari	207,805	2"291
4	R. Schumacher	Williams	207,549	8"803
5	D. Coulthard	McLaren	207,525	9"411
6	F. Alonso	Renault	206,192	43"689
7	J.P. Montoya	Williams	206,131	45"271
8	J. Button	BAR	204,500	1 lap
9	O. Panis	Toyota	203,778	1 lap
10	N. Heidfeld	Sauber	203,705	1 lap
11	H.H. Frentzen	Sauber	203,663	1 lap
12	C. Da Matta	Toyota	202,651	1 lap
13	J. Trulli	Renault	202,200	1 lap
14	A. Pizzonia	Jaguar	198,491	2 laps
15	G. Fisichella	Jordan	202,936	5 laps

RETIREMENTS

M. Webber	Jaguar	54	Axle-shaft
R. Firman	Jordan	51	Engine
J. Verstappen	Minardi	38	Electrical fault
J. Wilson	Minardi	23	Refuelling
J. Villeneuve	BAR	19	Hydraulic circuit

THE RACE

DRIVER	LAP	FASTEST LAP	AVERAGE SPEED (KPH)	TOP SPEED
M. Schumacher	17	1'22"491	215,281	310,500
R. Barrichello	49	1'22"775	214,543	310,300
K. Raikkonen	21	1'22"810	214,452	306,200
J.P. Montoya	32	1'22"946	214,100	308,400
D. Coulthard	20	1'23"200	213,447	306,300
R. Schumacher	29	1'23"265	213,280	307,600
F. Alonso	60	1'23"844	211,807	298,200
J. Button	15	1'23"972	211,484	303,300
J. Villeneuve	16	1'24"108	211,142	307,300
M. Webber	30	1'24"258	210,766	303,800
C. Da Matta	15	1'24"705	209,654	305,200
G. Fisichella	27	1'24"730	209,592	305,200
A. Pizzonia	36	1'24"733	209,585	304,900
H.H. Frentzen	34	1'24"874	209,237	303,200
O. Panis	36	1'25"123	208,625	302,500
N. Heidfeld	38	1'25"329	208,121	303,000
J. Trulli	13	1'25"444	207,841	296,400
R. Firman	45	1'25"539	207,610	299,800
J. Wilson	23	1'26"354	205,651	304,900
J. Verstappen	35	1'26"835	204,512	300,800

San Marino GP

THE CIRCUIT

20 April 2003
Circuit: Imola
Km.: 4,933
Laps: 62
Distance: 305,609 Kms

Schumacher takes dramatic win at Imola

Although Monza is the most famous Italian circuit in the world, Imola represents the Italian circuit par excellence. With Maranello just a quick drive down the autostrada and Minardi a stone's throw away, the Enzo & Dino Ferrari Circuit is the place where all of Italy comes to cheer on Italian teams and drivers.

Yet the 2003 race was held in a totally different atmosphere to the races of the past.

On Friday Giancarlo Fisichella was rewarded for his Brazilian GP win on the start-finish straight, with all the trappings of the podium ceremony, but in a surreal atmosphere due to a total lack of spectators.

This was followed the day after by the Schumacher brothers flying to their mother's deathbed in Cologne immediately after qualifying, in which they took the top two positions on the grid.

Michael and Ralf returned on Sunday morning, with that tragic loss in their hearts, to line up on the grid for what was probably their hardest race this season.

Ralf got off to a better start than his brother and led for 16 laps. The Williams driver only lost the lead during the first pit-stop on lap 16 after a slow getaway, and at that point his brother Michael hammered in a series of quick laps to annihilate the opposition.

The Ferrari driver kept the lead until the flag, only losing out during the next pit-stops which saw Raikkonen temporarily at the front.

It could have been a Ferrari 1-2 but in the final pit-stop Barrichello lost time with a wheel that failed to go on right. The Brazilian restarted in fourth place but powered past Ralf Schumacher with a superb move at the Variante Bassa to take the final podium slot. Second place remained in the hands of Raikkonen, who put in another steady drive.

Four races had produced four different winners but this time it was finally Michael Schumacher at the top of the podium for Ferrari's first 2003 victory … with the debut of the new F2003-GA still to come.

HIGHLIGHTS

After four races, one win, two seconds and a third place, 23 year-old Kimi Raikkonen was leading the championship. Considered a 'hothead' until last year, the 23 year-old Finn was now, at least for the media, a cold calculating 'iceman', both on and off the track. Kimi is tackling the 2003 championship with unprecedented determination, relegating the more expert Coulthard to number two driver.

PHOTO PORTFOLIO
PREVIOUS PAGES

Exchange of trophies between Raikkonen and Fisichella, who was awarded the first GP win of his career.
But it was Ferrari who won at their home circuit, with Schumacher first and Barrichello third.
The two Ferrari drivers sandwiched the surprise of the championship: Finland's Kimi Raikkonen with the McLaren.

	CHAMPIONSHIP POINTS	AUSTRALIAN GP	MALAYSIAN GP	BRAZILIAN GP	SAN MARINO GP	SPANISH GP	AUSTRIAN GP	MONACO GP	CANADIAN GP	EUROPEAN GP	FRENCH GP	BRITISH GP	GERMAN GP	HUNGARIAN GP	ITALIAN GP	UNITED STATES GP	JAPANESE GP	TOTAL POINTS
1	K. Raikkonen	6	10	8	8													32
2	D. Coulthard	10	-	5	4													19
3	M. Schumacher	5	3	-	10													18
4	F. Alonso	2	6	6	3													17
5	R. Barrichello	-	8	-	6													14
6	R. Schumacher	1	5	2	5													13
7	G. Fisichella	-	-	10	-													10
8	J.P. Montoya	8	-	-	2													10
9	J. Trulli	4	4	1	-													9
10	H.H. Frentzen	3	-	4	-													7
11	J. Villeneuve	-	-	3	-													3
12	J. Button	-	2	-	1													3
13	N. Heidfeld	-	1	-	-													1
14	M. Webber	-	-	-	-													0
15	A. Pizzonia	-	-	-	-													0
16	R. Firman	-	-	-	-													0
17	J. Verstappen	-	-	-	-													0
18	J. Wilson	-	-	-	-													0
19	O. Panis	-	-	-	-													0
20	C. Da Matta	-	-	-	-													0

POLE POSITION

2003 MICHAEL SCHUMACHER

'90	A. Senna
'91	G. Berger
'92	N. Mansell
'93	A. Prost
'94	M. Schumacher
'95	M. Schumacher
'96	D. Hill
'97	J. Villeneuve
'98	M. Hakkinen
'99	M. Hakkinen
'00	M. Schumacher
'01	M. Schumacher
'02	M. Schumacher

	1°	2°	3°
'90	A. Prost	N. Mansell	A. Nannini
'91	N. Mansell	A. Prost	R. Patrese
'92	N. Mansell	M. Schumacher	J. Alesi
'93	A. Prost	A. Senna	M. Schumacher
'94	D. Hill	M. Schumacher	M. Brundell
'95	M. Schumacher	J. Herbert	G. Berger
'96	M. Schumacher	J. Alesi	J. Villeneuve
'97	J. Villeneuve	O. Panis	J. Alesi
'98	M. Hakkinen	D. Coulthard	M. Schumacher
'99	M. Hakkinen	D. Coulthard	M. Schumacher
'00	M. Hakkinen	D. Coulthard	R. Barrichello
'01	M. Schumacher	J.P. Montoya	J. Villeneuve
'02	M. Schumacher	J.P. Montoya	D. Coulthard

STARTING GRID

MICHAEL SCHUMACHER
FERRARI
1'17"762

FERNANDO ALONSO
RENAULT
1'18"233

JENSON BUTTON
BAR
1'18"704

RALF SCHUMACHER
WILLIAMS
1'19"006

JUAN PABLO MONTOYA
WILLIAMS
1'19"377

JACQUES VILLENEUVE
BAR
1'19"563

CRISTIANO DA MATTA
TOYOTA
1'19"623

RALPH FIRMAN
JORDAN
1'20"215

GIANCARLO FISICHELLA
JORDAN
1'20"976

JOS VERSTAPPEN
MINARDI
1'22"237

RUBENS BARRICHELLO
FERRARI
1'18"020

JARNO TRULLI
RENAULT
1'18"615

OLIVIER PANIS
TOYOTA
1'18"811

DAVID COULTHARD
MCLAREN
1'19"128

H.HARALD FRENTZEN
SAUBER
1'19"427

MARK WEBBER
JAGUAR
1'19"615

NICK HEIDFELD
SAUBER
1'19"646

ANTONIO PIZZONIA
JAGUAR
1'20"308

JUSTIN WILSON
MINARDI
1'22"104

KIMI RAIKKONEN
MCLAREN

RESULTS

	DRIVER	CAR	KPH	GAP
1	M. Schumacher	Ferrari	196,619	-
2	F. Alonso	Renault	196,420	5"716
3	R. Barrichello	Ferrari	195,992	18"001
4	J.P. Montoya	Williams	194,476	1'02"022
5	R. Schumacher	Williams	193,289	1 lap
6	C. Da Matta	Toyota	193,277	1 lap
7	M. Webber	Jaguar	193,044	1 lap
8	R. Firman	Jordan	190,207	2 laps
9	J. Button	BAR	189,792	2 laps
10	N. Heidfeld	Sauber	189,761	2 laps
11	J. Wilson	Minardi	188,221	2 laps
12	J. Verstappen	Minardi	185,894	3 laps

RETIREMENTS

G. Fisichella	Jordan	43	Engine
O. Panis	Toyota	41	Gearbox
H.H. Frentzen	Sauber	38	Suspension
D. Coulthard	McLaren	17	Accident
J. Villeneuve	BAR	12	Electrical fault
J. Trulli	Renault	0	Accident
A. Pizzonia	Jaguar	0	Accident
K. Raikkonen	McLaren	0	Accident

THE RACE

DRIVER	LAP	FASTEST LAP	AVERAGE SPEED (KPH)	TOP SPEED
R. Barrichello	52	1'20"143	212,470	328,200
M. Schumacher	51	1'20"307	212,036	331,500
F. Alonso	42	1'20"476	211,591	317,600
R. Schumacher	8	1'20"798	210,747	319,100
O. Panis	14	1'20"803	210,734	324,200
C. Da Matta	22	1'20"935	210,391	323,600
J. Button	7	1'21"300	209,446	325,900
J.P. Montoya	21	1'21"448	209,065	320,800
H.H. Frentzen	32	1'21"791	208,189	320,100
M. Webber	20	1'21"967	207,742	323,400
J. Villeneuve	9	1'22"175	207,216	316,400
N. Heidfeld	34	1'22"568	206,230	323,100
D. Coulthard	10	1'22"577	206,207	327,900
R. Firman	29	1'22"719	205,853	317,800
G. Fisichella	17	1'22"900	205,404	320,100
J. Verstappen	16	1'22"942	205,300	317,600
J. Wilson	7	1'23"222	204,609	316,400
J. Trulli	-	-	-	-
A. Pizzonia	-	-	-	-
K. Raikkonen	-	-	-	-

Spanish GP

THE CIRCUIT

4 May 2003
Circuit: Barcelona
Km.: 4,730
Laps: 65
Distance: 307,324 Kms

Winning debut for F2003-GA

A multiple champion (Schumacher), a talented youngster (Alonso) and the brand-new Ferrari F2003-GA were the surprises of the Spanish weekend. First a mention for Alonso, who is increasingly setting the F1 world alight. His Renault might not be the most powerful around but it does have a superb-handling chassis and its Michelins are far superior to Bridgestones in warm conditions. But Ferrari is always Ferrari and the new GA could not have had a better debut, with a front-row qualifying position and two drivers on the podium.

The quickest getaway came from Alonso, thanks to Renault's electronic gizmos, and he tried to work his way in between the two Ferraris. Barrichello tried to resist into the first corner but his efforts were in vain. Out came the safety-car because at the back it was chaos. Pizzonia stalled at the start and was hit by Raikkonen while once again the unlucky Trulli was hit by Coulthard and they were both off the track. On the restart, the two Ferraris powered away, followed by the Spanish driver in the Renault. But on lap 20 Barrichello came in for his pit-stop and when he returned to the track he was behind Alonso, who in the meantime had put in a series of fastest laps, cheered on by a delirious local crowd.

The cheers turned into a Mexican wave when two-thirds into the race and after a second pit-stop, Alonso found himself ahead of Ralf Schumacher after a champion move under braking. But it was Schumacher who held onto first position until the flag, followed by Alonso, with the best result of his career, and by Barrichello. It could not have been a better debut for the new Ferrari F2003-GA. Sixth place went to Da Matta who scored Toyota's first points of the year.

HIGHLIGHTS

Alonso was clearly the man of the race at the Spanish track, scoring the third podium of the year. Finally Spanish fans had something to cheer about after years of uncompetitive drivers and scarce results. The last great Spanish hero was Alfonso de Portago in the 1950s, a gentleman-driver who finished second with a Lancia-Ferrari at Silverstone in 1956.

PHOTO PORTFOLIO
PREVIOUS PAGES

Ferrari scored the same two podium finishes again in Spain, this time sandwiching the new local hero, youngster Fernando Alonso. Photo at the foot of the page: his team-mate Trulli against the barriers on lap 1 after making contact with Coulthard.

	CHAMPIONSHIP POINTS	AUSTRALIAN GP	MALAYSIAN GP	BRAZILIAN GP	SAN MARINO GP	SPANISH GP	AUSTRIAN GP	MONACO GP	CANADIAN GP	EUROPEAN GP	FRENCH GP	BRITISH GP	GERMAN GP	HUNGARIAN GP	ITALIAN GP	UNITED STATES GP	JAPANESE GP	TOTAL POINTS
1	K. Raikkonen	6	10	8	8	-												32
2	M. Schumacher	5	3	-	10	10												28
3	F. Alonso	2	6	6	3	8												25
4	R. Barrichello	-	8	-	6	6												20
5	D. Coulthard	10	-	5	4	-												19
6	R. Schumacher	1	5	2	5	4												17
7	J.P. Montoya	8	-	-	2	5												15
8	G. Fisichella	-	-	10	-	-												10
9	J. Trulli	4	4	1	-	-												9
10	H.H. Frentzen	3	-	4	-	-												7
11	J. Villeneuve	-	-	3	-	-												3
12	C. Da Matta	-	-	-	-	3												3
13	J. Button	-	2	-	1	-												3
14	M. Webber	-	-	-	-	2												2
15	N. Heidfeld	-	1	-	-													1
16	R. Firman	-	-	-	-	1												1
17	A. Pizzonia	-	-	-	-													0
18	J. Verstappen	-	-	-	-													0
19	J. Wilson	-	-	-	-													0
20	O. Panis	-	-	-	-													0

POLE POSITION

2003 MICHAEL SCHUMACHER

	2	1	3
	1°	2°	3°

STARTING GRID

MICHAEL SCHUMACHER
FERRARI
1'09"150

JUAN PABLO MONTOYA
WILLIAMS
1'09"391

RUBENS BARRICHELLO
FERRARI
1'09"784

JENSON BUTTON
BAR
1'09"935

GIANCARLO FISICHELLA
JORDAN
1'10"105

OLIVIER PANIS
TOYOTA
1'10"402

CRISTIANO DA MATTA
TOYOTA
1'10"834

H.HARALD FRENTZEN
SAUBER
1'11"307

MARK WEBBER
JAGUAR
1'11"662

FERNANDO ALONSO
RENAULT
1'20"113

KIMI RAIKKONEN
MCLAREN
1'09"189

NICK HEIDFELD
SAUBER
1'09"725

JARNO TRULLI
RENAULT
1'09"890

ANTONIO PIZZONIA
JAGUAR
1'10"045

RALF SCHUMACHER
WILLIAMS
1'10"279

JACQUES VILLENEUVE
BAR
1'10"618

DAVID COULTHARD
MCLAREN
1'10"893

RALPH FIRMAN
JORDAN
1'11"505

JUSTIN WILSON
MINARDI
1'14"508

JOS VERSTAPPEN
MINARDI

RESULTS

	DRIVER	CAR	KPH	GAP
1	M. Schumacher	Ferrari	213,003	-
2	K. Raikkonen	McLaren	212,861	3"362
3	R. Barrichello	Ferrari	212,836	3"951
4	J. Button	BAR	211,234	42"243
5	D. Coulthard	McLaren	210,510	59"740
6	R. Schumacher	Williams	209,589	1 lap
7	M. Webber	Jaguar	209,300	1 lap
8	J. Trulli	Renault	208,504	1 lap
9	A. Pizzonia	Jaguar	208,270	1 lap
10	C. Da Matta	Toyota	208,012	1 lap
11	R. Firman	Jordan	207,845	1 lap
12	J. Villeneuve	BAR	207,817	1 lap
13	J. Wilson	Minardi	205,216	2 laps

RETIREMENTS

G. Fisichella	Jordan	60	Engine
N. Heidfeld	Sauber	46	Engine
F. Alonso	Renault	44	Engine
J.P. Montoya	Williams	32	Engine
O. Panis	Toyota	6	Suspension
J. Verstappen	Minardi	0	Electrical
H.H. Frentzen	Sauber	0	Clutch

THE RACE

DRIVER	LAP	FASTEST LAP	AVERAGE SPEED (KPH)	TOP SPEED
M. Schumacher	41	1'08"337	227,894	316,000
R. Barrichello	44	1'08"913	225,989	314,000
M. Webber	68	1'08"966	225,815	307,800
K. Raikkonen	45	1'09"423	224,329	308,200
D. Coulthard	64	1'09"626	223,675	310,700
J. Villeneuve	64	1'09"764	223,232	313,100
J. Button	22	1'09"828	223,028	310,800
A. Pizzonia	67	1'09"978	222,549	306,900
J.P. Montoya	28	1'10"112	222,124	309,600
R. Schumacher	40	1'10"246	221,700	312,000
J. Trulli	68	1'10"358	221,347	306,000
C. Da Matta	67	1'10"466	221,008	307,600
N. Heidfeld	12	1'10"516	220,852	307,500
F. Alonso	34	1'10"526	220,820	304,500
R. Firman	68	1'10"659	220,405	307,300
G. Fisichella	60	1'11"019	219,287	306,900
J. Wilson	67	1'11"267	218,524	303,000
O. Panis	6	1'13"097	213,053	302,600
J. Verstappen	-	-	-	-
H.H. Frentzen	-	-	-	-

Austrian GP

THE CIRCUIT

18 May 2003
Circuit: A1-Ring
Km.: 4,326
Laps: 71
Distance: 298,494 Kms

1-2-3 Schummy!

It was fitting that the greatest modern-day Formula 1 driver should draw the final curtain on the last Austrian GP to be held at the A1-Ring. Michael Schumacher not only set pole and took the eventual win after easily controlling his rivals, but left his name forever in the annals of the Austrian circuit which will no longer be a Formula 1 venue from 2004 onwards. The official reason, as in the case of Spa, is cigarette advertising, but the reality is that the A1-Ring is miles away from any major towns and cities, has few hotels and as a result the number of spectators is constantly dropping. In addition, dollar-rich China and Bahrain are knocking on the doors of Formula 1...
Schumacher was on pole position but at the lights da Matta stalled his Toyota and a restart was called. This time around da Matta stalled again and the start was aborted once more.

Meanwhile Frentzen attempted to switch to his spare Sauber but there wasn't enough time and he failed to line up for the restart. Verstappen also had a disastrous day after suffering problems with his Minardi during qualifying and then retiring 100 metres into the race with a launch-control glitch. Schumacher powered away followed by an aggressive Montoya and Raikkonen in third.
At the first round of pit-stops the number 1 Ferrari caught fire as the mechanics were removing the fuel hose from the car. Schumacher looked on imperturbably as the fire was extinguished. Half-way through the race Montoya retired with a blown engine while Schumacher succeeded in passing Raikkonen who had moved into the lead during the Ferrari driver's lengthy pit-stop.
Schumacher headed for his third successive win while Barrichello attempted to attack Raikkonen for second, but without success.

HIGHLIGHTS

Ralf Firman set nineteenth quickest time in Friday qualifying but it was the rear of his Jordan car that crossed the line first on his quick lap. The British driver came out of the final curve too quickly, went onto the grass and his Jordan spun backwards onto the straight and over the line.

PHOTO PORTFOLIO
PREVIOUS PAGES

While Fisichella shows off on his mountain-bike, Villeneuve waits disconsolately for the start at the side of the track.
Verstappen also has an off-day after stopping shortly after the start with electronic problems on his Minardi.

	CHAMPIONSHIP POINTS	AUSTRALIAN GP	MALAYSIAN GP	BRAZILIAN GP	SAN MARINO GP	SPANISH GP	AUSTRIAN GP	MONACO GP	CANADIAN GP	EUROPEAN GP	FRENCH GP	BRITISH GP	GERMAN GP	HUNGARIAN GP	ITALIAN GP	UNITED STATES GP	JAPANESE GP	TOTAL POINTS
1	K. Raikkonen	6	10	8	8	-	8											40
2	M. Schumacher	5	3	-	10	10	10											38
3	R. Barrichello	-	8	-	6	6	6											26
4	F. Alonso	2	6	6	3	8	-											25
5	D. Coulthard	10	-	5	4	-	4											23
6	R. Schumacher	1	5	2	5	4	3											20
7	J.P. Montoya	8	-	-	2	5	-											15
8	G. Fisichella	-	-	10	-	-	-											10
9	J. Trulli	4	4	1	-	-	1											10
10	J. Button	-	2	-	1	-	5											8
11	H.H. Frentzen	3	-	4	-	-	-											7
12	M. Webber	-	-	-	-	2	2											4
13	J. Villeneuve	-	-	3	-	-	-											3
14	C. Da Matta	-	-	-	-	3	-											3
15	N. Heidfeld	-	1	-	-	-	-											1
16	R. Firman	-	-	-	-	1	-											1
17	A. Pizzonia	-	-	-	-	-	-											0
18	J. Verstappen	-	-	-	-	-	-											0
19	J. Wilson	-	-	-	-	-	-											0
20	O. Panis	-	-	-	-	-	-											0

POLE POSITION

2003 RALF SCHUMACHER

'90	A. Senna
'91	A. Senna
'92	N. Mansell
'93	A. Prost
'94	M. Schumacher
'95	D. Hill
'96	M. Schumacher
'97	H.H. Frentzen
'98	M. Hakkinen
'99	M. Hakkinen
'00	M. Schumacher
'01	D. Coulthard
'02	J.P. Montoya

2 | **1** | **3**

	1°	2°	3°
'90	A. Senna	J. Alesi	G. Berger
'91	A. Senna	N. Mansell	J. Alesi
'92	A. Senna	N. Mansell	R. Patrese
'93	A. Senna	D. Hill	J. Alesi
'94	M. Schumacher	M. Brundle	G. Berger
'95	M. Schumacher	D. Hill	G. Berger
'96	O. Panis	D. Coulthard	J. Herbert
'97	M. Schumacher	R. Barrichello	E. Irvine
'98	M. Hakkinen	G. Fisichella	E. Irvine
'99	M. Schumacher	E. Irvine	M. Hakkinen
'00	D. Coulthard	R. Barrichello	G. Fisichella
'01	M. Schumacher	R. Barrichello	E. Irvine
'02	D. Coulthard	M. Schumacher	R. Schumacher

STARTING GRID

RALF SCHUMACHER
WILLIAMS
1'15"259

KIMI RAIKKONEN
McLAREN
1'15"295

JUAN PABLO MONTOYA
WILLIAMS
1'15"415

JARNO TRULLI
RENAULT
1'15"500

MICHAEL SCHUMACHER
FERRARI
1'15"644

DAVID COULTHARD
McLAREN
1'15"700

RUBENS BARRICHELLO
FERRARI
1'15"820

FERNANDO ALONSO
RENAULT
1'15"884

MARK WEBBER
JAGUAR
1'16"237

CRISTIANO DA MATTA
TOYOTA
1'16"744

JACQUES VILLENEUVE
BAR
1'16"755

GIANCARLO FISICHELLA
JORDAN
1'16"967

ANTONIO PIZZONIA
JAGUAR
1'17"103

NICK HEIDFELD
SAUBER
1'17"176

H.HARALD FRENTZEN
SAUBER
1'17"402

RALPH FIRMAN
JORDAN
1'17"452

OLIVIER PANIS
TOYOTA
1'17"464

JOS VERSTAPPEN
MINARDI
1'18"706

JUSTIN WILSON
MINARDI
1'20"063

RESULTS

	DRIVER	CAR	KPH	GAP
1	J.P. Montoya	Williams	152,772	-
2	K. Raikkonen	McLaren	152,757	0"602
3	M. Schumacher	Ferrari	152,729	1"720
4	R. Schumacher	Williams	152,066	28"518
5	F. Alonso	Renault	151,875	36"251
6	J. Trulli	Renault	151,759	40"972
7	D. Coulthard	McLaren	151,753	41"227
8	R. Barrichello	Ferrari	151,458	53"266
9	C. Da Matta	Toyota	149,221	1 lap
10	G. Fisichella	Jordan	149,185	1 lap
11	N. Heidfeld	Sauber	148,291	2 laps
12	R. Firman	Jordan	147,685	2 laps
13	O. Panis	Toyota	143,815	3 laps

RETIREMENTS

J. Villeneuve	BAR	63	Engine
J. Wilson	Minardi	29	Engine
J. Verstappen	Minardi	28	Engine
M. Webber	Jaguar	16	Engine
A. Pizzonia	Jaguar	10	Electrical fault
H.H. Frentzen	Sauber	0	Crashed

THE RACE

DRIVER	LAP	FASTEST LAP	AVERAGE SPEED (KPH)	TOP SPEED
K. Raikkonen	49	1'14"545	161,298	300,900
M. Schumacher	30	1'14"707	160,948	300,000
R. Schumacher	77	1'14"768	160,817	298,400
J.P. Montoya	47	1'14"902	160,529	298,000
R. Barrichello	59	1'15"307	159,666	299,700
F. Alonso	58	1'15"397	159,475	289,000
D. Coulthard	51	1'15"439	159,387	300,400
J. Trulli	51	1'15"679	158,881	287,900
C. Da Matta	51	1'16"282	157,625	295,000
J. Villeneuve	50	1'16"292	157,604	295,800
G. Fisichella	72	1'16"647	156,875	290,200
N. Heidfeld	75	1'16"835	156,491	291,400
R. Firman	51	1'17"208	155,735	292,300
O. Panis	70	1'17"777	154,595	290,600
M. Webber	13	1'18"004	154,145	292,800
J. Verstappen	25	1'19"146	151,921	291,700
J. Wilson	19	1'19"169	151,877	288,000
A. Pizzonia	8	1'19"437	151,365	294,100
H.H. Frentzen	-	-	-	-
J. Button	-	-	-	-

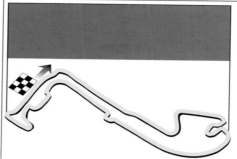

Monaco GP

THE CIRCUIT

1 June 2003
Circuit: Montecarlo
Km.: 3,340
Laps: 78
Distance: 260,520 Kms

Triumph for Williams and Michelin

Ralf Schumacher set pole for the Monte Carlo race, followed by Raikkonen, team-mate Montoya and Trulli.

Schumacher could only set fifth quickest time and Barrichello seventh. Ralf took the lead, followed by Montoya who passed both Raikkonen and Trulli after a superb start.

The two Williams continued at a terrific pace up front, with Ralf unsuccessfully trying to pull away from his team-mate before the first pit-stop. It was the German who came in first, on lap 21, followed by the Colombian two laps later, but it was Montoya who came out ahead of the German.

Behind, Michael Schumacher was finding it difficult to overtake Trulli who was entirely at ease around the Monte Carlo streets. Thanks to the pit-stops Schummy managed to pass the Italian driver to slot into third place behind Montoya and Raikkonen.

The race moved towards its inevitable conclusion and Montoya picked up his first win of 2003 from Raikkonen, who scored some useful points to hold onto his lead in the championship. Alonso was also in the points again after a steady race that took him to fifth at the flag.

Barrichello was off-form, the Brazilian failing to make up any places during the race, while Ralf Schumacher slipped down to fourth at the flag after his good start from pole position. Frentzen had another poor race, the German failing to complete a lap for the second time in succession. In Austria HH stalled, while at Monte Carlo the German crashed his Sauber into the guard rail at the Swimming Pool on the first lap.

HIGHLIGHTS

The key talking-point at Monte Carlo was the fact that there wasn't any overtaking, even amongst the backmarkers. For statistics lovers, this is the first time it has happened in eleven years, but for everyone else watching on TV and around the Principality track the race offered a pretty poor show.

PHOTO PORTFOLIO
PREVIOUS PAGES

Montoya picked up a superb win on this tricky street circuit, which was not thought to be suitable for his particular driving style. In the photo sequence, Button's crash, which caused him to miss the Monaco GP after medical officers ruled him to be unfit.

CHAMPIONSHIP POINTS		AUSTRALIAN GP	MALAYSIAN GP	BRAZILIAN GP	SAN MARINO GP	SPANISH GP	AUSTRIAN GP	MONACO GP	CANADIAN GP	EUROPEAN GP	FRENCH GP	BRITISH GP	GERMAN GP	HUNGARIAN GP	ITALIAN GP	UNITED STATES GP	JAPANESE GP	TOTAL POINTS
1	K. Raikkonen	6	10	8	8	-	8	8										48
2	M. Schumacher	5	3	-	10	10	10	6										44
3	F. Alonso	2	6	6	3	8	-	4										29
4	R. Barrichello	-	8	-	6	6	6	1										27
5	D. Coulthard	10	-	5	4	-	4	2										25
6	J.P. Montoya	8	-	-	2	5	-	10										25
7	R. Schumacher	1	5	2	5	4	3	5										25
8	J. Trulli	4	4	1	-	-	1	3										13
9	G. Fisichella	-	-	10	-	-	-	-										10
10	J. Button	-	2	-	1	-	5	-										8
11	H.H. Frentzen	3	-	4	-	-	-	-										7
12	M. Webber	-	-	-	-	2	2	-										4
13	J. Villeneuve	-	-	3	-	-	-	-										3
14	C. Da Matta	-	-	-	-	3	-	-										3
15	N. Heidfeld	-	1	-	-	-	-	-										1
16	R. Firman	-	-	-	-	1	-	-										1
17	A. Pizzonia	-	-	-	-	-	-	-										0
18	J. Verstappen	-	-	-	-	-	-	-										0
19	J. Wilson	-	-	-	-	-	-	-										0
20	O. Panis	-	-	-	-	-	-	-										0

POLE POSITION

2003
RALF SCHUMACHER

'90	A. Senna
'91	R. Patrese
'92	A. Senna
'93	A. Prost
'94	M. Schumacher
'95	M. Schumacher
'96	D. Hill
'97	M. Schumacher
'98	D. Coulthard
'99	M. Schumacher
'00	M. Schumacher
'01	M. Schumacher
'02	J.P. Montoya

2 **1** **3**

	1°	2°	3°
'90	A. Senna	N. Piquet	N. Mansell
'91	N. Piquet	S. Modena	R. Patrese
'92	G. Berger	M. Schumacher	J. Alesi
'93	A. Prost	M. Schumacher	D. Hill
'94	M. Schumacher	D. Hill	J. Alesi
'95	J. Alesi	R. Barrichello	E. Irvine
'96	D. Hill	J. Villeneuve	J. Alesi
'97	M. Schumacher	J. Alesi	G. Fisichella
'98	M. Schumacher	G. Fisichella	E. Irvine
'99	M. Hakkinen	G. Fisichella	E. Irvine
'00	M. Schumacher	R. Barrichello	G. Fisichella
'01	R. Schumacher	M. Schumacher	M. Hakkinen
'02	M. Schumacher	D. Coulthard	R. Barrichello

STARTING GRID

 RALF SCHUMACHER
WILLIAMS
1'15"529

 JUAN PABLO MONTOYA
WILLIAMS
1'15"923

 MICHAEL SCHUMACHER
FERRARI
1'16"047

 FERNANDO ALONSO
RENAULT
1'16"048

 RUBENS BARRICHELLO
FERRARI
1'16"143

 MARK WEBBER
JAGUAR
1'16"182

 OLIVIER PANIS
TOYOTA
1'16"598

 JARNO TRULLI
RENAULT
1'16"718

 CRISTIANO DA MATTA
TOYOTA
1'16"826

 H.HARALD FRENTZEN
SAUBER
1'16"939

 DAVID COULTHARD
McLAREN
1'17"024

 NICK HEIDFELD
SAUBER
1'17"086

 ANTONIO PIZZONIA
JAGUAR
1'17"337

 JACQUES VILLENEUVE
BAR
1'17"347

 JOS VERSTAPPEN
MINARDI
1'18"014

 GIANCARLO FISICHELLA
JORDAN
1'18"036

 JENSON BUTTON
BAR
1'18"205

 JUSTIN WILSON
MINARDI
1'18"560

 RALPH FIRMAN
JORDAN
1'18"692

 KIMI RAIKKONEN
McLAREN

RESULTS

	DRIVER	CAR	KPH	GAP
1	M. Schumacher	Ferrari	200,777	-
2	R. Schumacher	Williams	200,748	0"784
3	J.P. Montoya	Williams	200,727	1"355
4	F. Alonso	Renault	200,612	4"481
5	R. Barrichello	Ferrari	198,447	1'04"261
6	K. Raikkonen	McLaren	198,223	1'10"502
7	M. Webber	Jaguar	196,767	1 lap
8	O. Panis	Toyota	196,252	1 lap
9	J. Verstappen	Minardi	193,586	2 laps
10	A. Pizzonia	Jaguar	191,784	4 laps
11	C. Da Matta	Toyota	196,524	6 laps

RETIREMENTS

J. Wilson	Minardi	60	Gearbox
J. Button	BAR	51	Gearbox
D. Coulthard	McLaren	47	Gearbox
N. Heidfeld	Sauber	47	Engine
J. Trulli	Renault	22	Accident
G. Fisichella	Jordan	20	Gearbox
R. Firman	Jordan	20	Engine
J. Villeneuve	BAR	14	Brakes
H.H. Frentzen	Sauber	6	Electrical

THE RACE

DRIVER	LAP	FASTEST LAP	AVERAGE SPEED (KPH)	TOP SPEED
F. Alonso	53	1'16"040	206,465	338,900
J.P. Montoya	39	1'16"349	205,629	342,400
R. Barrichello	35	1'16"368	205,578	344,800
M. Schumacher	46	1'16"378	205,551	348,400
R. Schumacher	48	1'16"599	204,958	341,800
K. Raikkonen	67	1'16"699	204,691	345,000
D. Coulthard	23	1'17"088	203,658	343,200
G. Fisichella	20	1'17"186	203,399	334,200
A. Pizzonia	54	1'17"324	203,036	329,200
J. Button	22	1'17"562	202,413	339,900
M. Webber	45	1'17"592	202,335	331,000
N. Heidfeld	44	1'17"769	201,874	333,600
C. Da Matta	38	1'17"787	201,828	338,600
O. Panis	40	1'17"904	201,524	335,700
J. Wilson	42	1'18"039	201,176	333,000
J. Verstappen	38	1'18"521	199,941	334,400
J. Trulli	16	1'18"696	199,496	332,300
R. Firman	18	1'19"453	197,596	326,400
J. Villeneuve	6	1'19"780	196,786	338,200
H.H. Frentzen	3	1'20"043	196,139	337,000

Canadian GP

THE CIRCUIT

15 June 2003
Circuit: Montreal
Km.: 4,361
Laps: 70
Distance: 305,270 Kms

Red is the colour in Canada and Spain

This particular Sunday saw a historic double triumph for Italian colours and in particular the scarlet red-liveried Ferrari and Ducati. In Spain Loris Capirossi and Ducati won their maiden MotoGP race, the first time in almost 30 years (since Agostini on the MV-Agusta in 1976) an Italian rider and bike had taken the top honours. In Canada there was an all-family battle between the Schumacher brothers. Ralf again set pole (after Monte Carlo) while Michael won from his brother, Montoya and the increasingly competitive Alonso. It was not an easy GP for Ferrari,

who seemed outclassed by Williams in qualifying but whose task was then made easier in the race by the errors of their rivals. Ralf Schumacher failed to increase his lead over his brother on a clear track in the early stages of the race, and then lost out during the pit-stop phase with a slow entry and exit. Montoya ruined his chances of a win with a mistake on the second lap. Barrichello also had a bad race to finish fifth, after his nervous start had led him to hit the rear of Alonso's Renault, bending the front wing of his Ferrari. Dutchman Jos Verstappen was out of luck, missing out on eighth place and one point after setting an excellent fifteenth quickest time in Saturday qualifying.

HIGHLIGHTS

Paul Stoddart, the Minardi boss, went on the warpath in Canada. His particular target was Bernie Ecclestone, and the Australian was claiming a greater share of the F1 money for his team. In reply a few days later Bernie announced he had bought up part of the shares of the Minardi team! This was a breath of fresh air for the coffers of the Italian squad, which has always been in search of a major sponsorship deal.

PHOTO PORTFOLIO
PREVIOUS PAGES

The Schumacher brothers on the Canadian GP podium with third-placed Montoya.
On the other page, Frentzen's crash in qualifying with his Sauber and Dutchman Verstappen with the Minardi, who just finished out of the points after a superb race.

	CHAMPIONSHIP POINTS	AUSTRALIAN GP	MALAYSIAN GP	BRAZILIAN GP	SAN MARINO GP	SPANISH GP	AUSTRIAN GP	MONACO GP	CANADIAN GP	EUROPEAN GP	FRENCH GP	BRITISH GP	GERMAN GP	HUNGARIAN GP	ITALIAN GP	UNITED STATES GP	JAPANESE GP	TOTAL POINTS
1	M. Schumacher	5	3	-	10	10	10	6	10									54
2	K. Raikkonen	6	10	8	8	-	8	8	3									51
3	F. Alonso	2	6	6	3	8	-	4	5									34
4	R. Schumacher	1	5	2	5	4	3	5	8									33
5	J.P. Montoya	8	-	-	2	5	-	10	6									31
6	R. Barrichello	-	8	-	6	6	6	1	4									31
7	D. Coulthard	10	-	5	4	-	4	2	-									25
8	J. Trulli	4	4	1	-	-	1	3	-									13
9	G. Fisichella	-	-	10	-	-	-	-	-									10
10	J. Button	-	2	-	1	-	5	-	-									8
11	H.H. Frentzen	3	-	4	-	-	-	-	-									7
12	M. Webber	-	-	-	-	2	2	-	2									6
13	J. Villeneuve	-	-	3	-	-	-	-	-									3
14	C. Da Matta	-	-	-	-	3	-	-	-									3
15	N. Heidfeld	-	1	-	-	-	-	-	-									1
16	R. Firman	-	-	-	-	1	-	-	-									1
17	O. Panis	-	-	-	-	-	-	-	1									1
18	A. Pizzonia	-	-	-	-	-	-	-	-									0
19	J. Verstappen	-	-	-	-	-	-	-	-									0
20	J. Wilson	-	-	-	-	-	-	-	-									0

POLE POSITION

2003
KIMI
RAIKKONEN

Year	Pole
'90	-
'91	-
'92	-
'93	A. Prost
'94	M. Schumacher
'95	D. Coulthard
'96	D. Hill
'97	J. Villeneuve
'98	-
'99	H.H. Frentzen
'00	D. Coulthard
'01	M. Schumacher
'02	J.P. Montoya

2 **1** **3**

	1°	2°	3°
'90	-	-	-
'91	-	-	-
'92	-	-	-
'93	A. Senna	D. Hill	A. Prost
'94	M. Schumacher	D. Hill	M. Hakkinen
'95	M. Schumacher	J. Alesi	D. Coulthard
'96	J. Villeneuve	M. Schumacher	D. Coulthard
'97	M. Hakkinen	D. Coulthard	J. Villeneuve
'98	-	-	-
'99	J. Herbert	J. Trulli	R. Barrichello
'00	M. Schumacher	M. Hakkinen	D. Coulthard
'01	M. Schumacher	J.P. Montoya	D. Coulthard
'02	R. Barrichello	M. Schumacher	K. Raikkonen

STARTING GRID

 KIMI RAIKKONEN
McLAREN
1'31"523

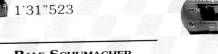 **MICHAEL SCHUMACHER**
FERRARI
1'31"555

 RALF SCHUMACHER
WILLIAMS
1'31"619

 JUAN PABLO MONTOYA
WILLIAMS
1'31"765

 RUBENS BARRICHELLO
FERRARI
1'31"780

 JARNO TRULLI
RENAULT
1'31"976

 OLIVIER PANIS
TOYOTA
1'32"350

 FERNANDO ALONSO
RENAULT
1'32"424

 DAVID COULTHARD
McLAREN
1'32"742

 CRISTIANO DA MATTA
TOYOTA
1'32"949

 MARK WEBBER
JAGUAR
1'33"066

 JENSON BUTTON
BAR
1'33"395

 GIANCARLO FISICHELLA
JORDAN
1'33"553

 RALPH FIRMAN
JORDAN
1'33"827

 H.HARALD FRENTZEN
SAUBER
1'34"000

 ANTONIO PIZZONIA
JAGUAR
1'34"159

 JACQUES VILLENEUVE
BAR
1'34"596

 JOS VERSTAPPEN
MINARDI
1'36"318

 JUSTIN WILSON
MINARDI
1'36"485

 NICK HEIDFELD
SAUBER

RESULTS

	DRIVER	CAR	KPH	GAP
1	R. Schumacher	Williams	195,633	-
2	J.P. Montoya	Williams	195,056	16"821
3	R. Barrichello	Ferrari	194,277	39"673
4	F. Alonso	Renault	193,396	1'05"731
5	M. Schumacher	Ferrari	193,382	1'06"162
6	M. Webber	Jaguar	192,014	1 lap
7	J. Button	BAR	191,509	1 lap
8	N. Heidfeld	Sauber	190,779	1 lap
9	H.H. Frentzen	Sauber	190,147	1 lap
10	A. Pizzonia	Jaguar	190,124	1 lap
11	R. Firman	Jordan	188,456	2 laps
12	G. Fisichella	Jordan	187,658	2 laps
13	J. Wilson	Minardi	186,833	2 laps
14	J. Verstappen	Minardi	185,040	3 laps
15	D. Coulthard	McLaren	193,452	4 laps

RETIREMENTS

C. Da Matta	Toyota	53	Engine
J. Villeneuve	BAR	51	Gearbox
J. Trulli	Renault	37	Fuel pressure
O. Panis	Toyota	37	Brakes
K. Raikkonen	McLaren	25	Engine

THE RACE

DRIVER	LAP	FASTEST LAP	AVERAGE SPEED (KPH)	TOP SPEED
K. Raikkonen	14	1'32"621	195,584	308,100
R. Schumacher	34	1'32"826	195,633	312,800
M. Schumacher	34	1'32"904	193,382	311,200
J.P. Montoya	59	1'33"094	195,056	313,100
R. Barrichello	15	1'33"200	194,277	310,700
D. Coulthard	12	1'33"236	193,452	311,900
F. Alonso	17	1'33"307	193,396	307,300
J. Trulli	13	1'33"348	194,378	307,100
C. Da Matta	15	1'33"398	189,981	312,900
O. Panis	8	1'33"583	190,766	309,300
H.H. Frentzen	33	1'33"994	190,147	308,600
M. Webber	37	1'34"191	192,014	306,600
J. Button	14	1'34"208	191,509	307,600
N. Heidfeld	23	1'34"541	190,779	311,400
G. Fisichella	29	1'34"656	187,658	305,300
A. Pizzonia	47	1'34"915	190,124	307,700
J. Villeneuve	45	1'35"100	187,974	310,200
R. Firman	29	1'35"328	188,456	304,500
J. Wilson	19	1'36"709	186,833	310,700
J. Verstappen	3	1'37"365	185,040	301,000

European GP

THE CIRCUIT

29 June 2003
Circuit: Nürburgring
Km.: 5,148
Laps: 60
Distance: 308,863 Kms

Williams 1-2, McLaren disaster!

Things looked to be going well for Kimi Raikkonen, who was the quickest in Friday pre-qualifying as well as on Saturday to take the first pole position of his career.

The Finn got off to a perfect start and was the undisputed leader until lap 25 of the 60-lap race when his Mercedes engine exploded, leaving the way clear for the other title pretenders. Williams then took over the top 2 positions, with Ralf Schumacher ahead of Montoya who was in the midst of yet another duel with Schumacher. The Colombian made a spectacular overtaking move on Schumacher, forcing the Ferrari driver into a spin and an off-track excursion that lost him a few places. While Ralf had things easy up front ahead of Montoya, Barrichello and Alonso moved into third and fourth, followed by Coulthard who made a number of unsuccessful attacks on the young Spanish driver. Alonso even recklessly braked early into one curve, forcing Coulthard to take evasive action and go off the track.

Meanwhile Schumacher had moved up to fifth place and in turn tried to attack Alonso, who once again held on to the points-scoring place by the skin of his teeth.

Sixth was Webber with the Jaguar, followed by Button (BAR) and Heidfeld (Sauber), who had starter the race from the pits after switching cars. McLaren's disastrous race was completed with the fifteenth and last place for Coulthard, who had been slow in qualifying and who was left behind by his young Finish team-mate. It is true that Alonso surprised him with an early braking manoeuvre, but a driver of his experience should not have fallen into the Spanish trap so easily.

HIGHLIGHTS

Kimi Raikkonen was again the talking point of the race after dominating the weekend but the Finn retired while heading for an easy win. Except for the Spanish GP when he crashed into Pizzonia's Jaguar at the start, Kimi has terminated all the other races this year in the points with six podium finishes.

PHOTO PORTFOLIO
PREVIOUS PAGES

150 GPs for David Coulthard, who celebrates in the McLaren pits, but it wasn't to be the best of weekends for the Scottish driver as he finished last after going off the circuit while battling with Alonso.

The two Williams drivers on the top of the podium and Ralf Schumacher's first win in 2003.

CHAMPIONSHIP POINTS		AUSTRALIAN GP	MALAYSIAN GP	BRAZILIAN GP	SAN MARINO GP	SPANISH GP	AUSTRIAN GP	MONACO GP	CANADIAN GP	EUROPEAN GP	FRENCH GP	BRITISH GP	GERMAN GP	HUNGARIAN GP	ITALIAN GP	UNITED STATES GP	JAPANESE GP	TOTAL POINTS
1	M. Schumacher	5	3	-	10	10	10	6	10	4								58
2	K. Raikkonen	6	10	8	8	-	8	8	3	-								51
3	R. Schumacher	1	5	2	5	4	3	5	8	10								43
4	J.P. Montoya	8	-	-	2	5	-	10	6	8								39
5	F. Alonso	2	6	6	3	8	-	4	5	5								39
6	R. Barrichello	-	8	-	6	6	6	1	4	6								37
7	D. Coulthard	10	-	5	4	-	4	2	-	-								25
8	J. Trulli	4	4	1	-	-	1	3	-	-								13
9	G. Fisichella	-	-	10	-	-	-	-	-	-								10
10	J. Button	-	2	-	1	-	5	-	-	2								10
11	M. Webber	-	-	-	-	2	2	-	2	3								9
12	H.H. Frentzen	3	-	4	-	-	-	-	-	-								7
13	J. Villeneuve	-	-	3	-	-	-	-	-	-								3
14	C. Da Matta	-	-	-	-	3	-	-	-	-								3
15	N. Heidfeld	-	1	-	-	-	-	-	-	1								2
16	R. Firman	-	-	-	-	1	-	-	-	-								1
17	O. Panis	-	-	-	-	-	-	-	1	-								1
18	A. Pizzonia	-	-	-	-	-	-	-	-	-								0
19	J. Verstappen	-	-	-	-	-	-	-	-	-								0
20	J. Wilson	-	-	-	-	-	-	-	-	-								0

VILLENEUVE
Jacques

BUTTON
Jenson

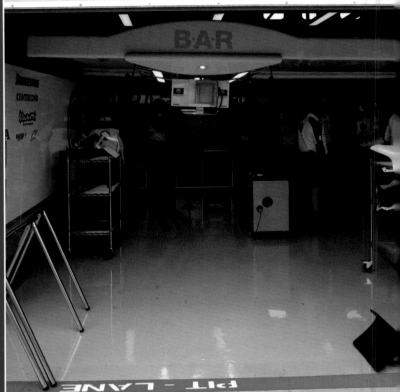

OBJETS SAISIS

PAR LA S.C.P.
ETIENNE LAMOTTE
BRUNO GYS
ANDRE WAGNER

HUISSIERS DE JUSTICE
ASSOCIES
2 AVENUE SAINT JUST
58000 NEVERS

IMPORTANT :

Article 314-6 du Code Pénal
Le fait, par le soin, de détruire ou de détourner un objet saisi entre en mains en garantie des droits d'un créancier et confié à sa garde ou à celle d'un tiers est puni de trois ans d'emprisonnement et de 375000 Euros d'amende.
La tentative de l'infraction prévue au présent article est punie des mêmes peines.

Article 434-22 du Code Pénal
Le bris de scellés apposés par l'autorité publique est puni de deux ans d'emprisonnement et de 30000 Euros d'amende. La tentative de bris de scellés est punie des mêmes peines.
Le fait des mêmes peine tout détournement d'objet placé sous scellés ou sous main de justice.

POLE POSITION

2003
RALF SCHUMACHER

'90	N. Mansell
'91	R. Patrese
'92	N. Mansell
'93	D. Hill
'94	D. Hill
'95	D. Hill
'96	M. Schumacher
'97	M. Schumacher
'98	M. Hakkinen
'99	R. Barrichello
'00	M. Schumacher
'01	R. Schumacher
'02	J.P. Montoya

2 **1** **3**

1°	2°	3°
'90	A. Prost	I. Capelli	A. Senna
'91	N. Mansell	A. Prost	A. Senna
'92	N. Mansell	A. Prost	M. Brundle
'93	A. Prost	D. Hill	M. Schumacher
'94	M. Schumacher	D. Hill	G. Berger
'95	M. Schumacher	D. Hill	D. Coulthard
'96	D. Hill	J. Villeneuve	J. Alesi
'97	M. Schumacher	H.H. Frentzen	E. Irvine
'98	M. Schumacher	E. Irvine	M. Hakkinen
'99	H.H. Frentzen	M. Hakkinen	R. Barrichello
'00	D. Coulthard	M. Hakkinen	R. Barrichello
'01	M. Schumacher	R. Schumacher	R. Barrichello
'02	M. Schumacher	K. Raikkonen	D. Coulthard

STARTING GRID

RALF SCHUMACHER
WILLIAMS
1'15"019

MICHAEL SCHUMACHER
FERRARI
1'15"480

DAVID COULTHARD
McLAREN
1'15"628

FERNANDO ALONSO
RENAULT
1'16"087

MARK WEBBER
JAGUAR
1'16"308

ANTONIO PIZZONIA
JAGUAR
1'16"965

CRISTIANO DA MATTA
TOYOTA
1'17"068

NICK HEIDFELD
SAUBER
1'17"445

GIANCARLO FISICHELLA
JORDAN
1'18"431

JOS VERSTAPPEN
MINARDI
1'18"709

JUAN PABLO MONTOYA
WILLIAMS
1'15"136

KIMI RAIKKONEN
McLAREN
1'15"533

JARNO TRULLI
RENAULT
1'15"967

RUBENS BARRICHELLO
FERRARI
1'16"166

OLIVIER PANIS
TOYOTA
1'16"345

JACQUES VILLENEUVE
BAR
1'16"990

JENSON BUTTON
BAR
1'17"077

H.HARALD FRENTZEN
SAUBER
1'17"562

RALPH FIRMAN
JORDAN
1'18"514

JUSTIN WILSON
MINARDI
1'19"619

RESULTS

	DRIVER	CAR	KPH	GAP
1	R. Schumacher	Williams	203,866	-
2	J.P. Montoya	Williams	203,350	13"813
3	M. Schumacher	Ferrari	203,136	19"568
4	K. Raikkonen	McLaren	202,452	38"047
5	D. Coulthard	McLaren	202,369	40"289
6	M. Webber	Jaguar	201,412	1'06"380
7	R. Barrichello	Ferrari	200,917	1 lap
8	O. Panis	Toyota	200,292	1 lap
9	J. Villeneuve	BAR	199,367	1 lap
10	A. Pizzonia	Jaguar	199,335	1 lap
11	C. Da Matta	Toyota	199,051	1 lap
12	H.H. Frentzen	Sauber	197,640	2 laps
13	N. Heidfeld	Sauber	196,790	2 laps
14	J. Wilson	Minardi	194,763	3 laps
15	R. Firman	Jordan	193,628	3 laps
16	J. Verstappen	Minardi	190,566	4 laps

RETIREMENTS

J. Trulli	Renault	45	Electrical
F. Alonso	Renault	43	Engine
G. Fisichella	Jordan	42	Engine
J. Button	BAR	21	Fuel pressure

THE RACE

DRIVER	LAP	FASTEST LAP	AVERAGE SPEED (KPH)	TOP SPEED
J.P. Montoya	36	1'15"512	203,350	318,400
R. Schumacher	37	1'15"698	203,866	319,600
D. Coulthard	17	1'15"981	202,369	316,400
M. Schumacher	19	1'16"303	203,136	322,400
K. Raikkonen	19	1'16"609	202,452	315,800
J. Trulli	33	1'17"025	199,251	308,300
F. Alonso	11	1'17"029	201,672	311,800
M. Webber	47	1'17"068	201,412	313,200
R. Barrichello	47	1'17"104	200,917	322,400
J. Button	19	1'17"149	197,688	315,800
O. Panis	36	1'17"398	200,292	314,500
A. Pizzonia	67	1'17"416	199,335	311,000
J. Villeneuve	49	1'17"786	199,367	314,100
C. Da Matta	63	1'17"870	199,051	312,300
H.H. Frentzen	18	1'18"099	197,640	313,300
J. Verstappen	66	1'18"754	190,566	309,400
N. Heidfeld	21	1'18"994	196,790	310,700
G. Fisichella	23	1'19"093	196,294	307,600
R. Firman	13	1'19"345	193,628	308,500
J. Wilson	25	1'19"588	194,763	306,500

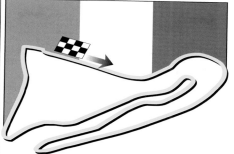

French GP

THE CIRCUIT

6 July 2003
Circuit: Magny-Cours
Km.: 4,411
Laps: 70
Distance: 308,586 Kms

Verstappen 'takes' pole!

The Ferrari pit garage went crazy in the last few minutes of Friday qualifying when Jos Verstappen (Minardi) took to the track at the same time as it stopped raining. The cheers then turned into a long and sincere applause when the Dutch driver set provisional pole. Michael Schumacher, a great friend of Jos, jokingly hoped that Minardi would repeat the performance on Saturday. This would have been just recognition for the smallest and most-loved team in the paddock.

But the miracle was not repeated on Saturday and the two Williams locked out the front row, with Ralf on pole, followed by Montoya, Schumacher (Ferrari), the two McLarens and the Renaults.

Ralf powered away from the lights with Montoya tucked in behind and immediately started to pull away while Barrichello, who started in eighth position, had a spin at the end of the first lap and was relegated to the back of the field. Schumacher was passed by Raikkonen at the start but from that point onwards he ran a superb race despite the fact that his Ferrari was clearly inferior to the two Williams and perhaps even to the two McLarens, which had improved since the Europe GP.

After his second pit-stop in fact Schumacher was behind the two McLarens but he then put in a series of extraordinary laps, passing the back-markers with authority. He even ran the risk of delaying his final pit-stop for a few laps and this proved to be the ideal strategy. When he returned to the track, the two McLarens were behind him. The GP came to an end without any further surprises, with Ralf ahead of Montoya and his brother, followed by the two McLarens, the Jaguar of Webber, an off-form Barrichello and Panis, who picked up his second point of the season.

HIGHLIGHTS

Thirty-one year-old Jos Verstappen from the Netherlands, who is in his eighth year in Formula 1, notched up the 100 GP mark in France. Friday's provisional pole, which came about purely by chance due to the adverse weather conditions, helped him and Minardi hit the front page of the international press.
At the end of Friday's session, almost all the F1 teams and colleagues went over to congratulate him in the Minardi pit garage.
This was a rare moment of satisfaction for the Faenza-based team, which was founded by Giancarlo Minardi and which is now run by Paul Stoddart.

PHOTO PORTFOLIO
PREVIOUS PAGES

Much ado about nothing for BAR on GP Friday, when the bailiffs temporarily confiscated the cars.
Page alongside: Trulli's retirement and Ralf Schumacher arrives in triumph.

	CHAMPIONSHIP POINTS	AUSTRALIAN GP	MALAYSIAN GP	BRAZILIAN GP	SAN MARINO GP	SPANISH GP	AUSTRIAN GP	MONACO GP	CANADIAN GP	EUROPEAN GP	FRENCH GP	BRITISH GP	GERMAN GP	HUNGARIAN GP	ITALIAN GP	UNITED STATES GP	JAPANESE GP	TOTAL POINTS
1	M. Schumacher	5	3	-	10	10	10	6	10	4	6							64
2	K. Raikkonen	6	10	8	8	-	8	8	3	-	5							56
3	R. Schumacher	1	5	2	5	4	3	5	8	10	10							53
4	J.P. Montoya	8	-	-	2	5	-	10	6	8	8							47
5	F. Alonso	2	6	6	3	8	-	4	5	5	-							39
6	R. Barrichello	-	8	-	6	6	6	1	4	6	2							39
7	D. Coulthard	10	-	5	4	-	4	2	-	-	4							29
8	J. Trulli	4	4	1	-	-	1	3	-	-	-							13
9	M. Webber	-	-	-	-	2	2	-	2	3	3							12
10	G. Fisichella	-	-	10	-	-	-	-	-	-	-							10
11	J. Button	-	2	-	1	-	5	-	-	2	-							10
12	H.H. Frentzen	3	-	4	-	-	-	-	-	-	-							7
13	J. Villeneuve	-	-	3	-	-	-	-	-	-	-							3
14	C. Da Matta	-	-	-	-	3	-	-	-	-	-							3
15	N. Heidfeld	-	1	-	-	-	-	-	-	1	-							2
16	O. Panis	-	-	-	-	-	-	-	1	-	1							2
17	R. Firman	-	-	-	-	1	-	-	-	-	-							1
18	A. Pizzonia	-	-	-	-	-	-	-	-	-	-							0
19	J. Verstappen	-	-	-	-	-	-	-	-	-	-							0
20	J. Wilson	-	-	-	-	-	-	-	-	-	-							0

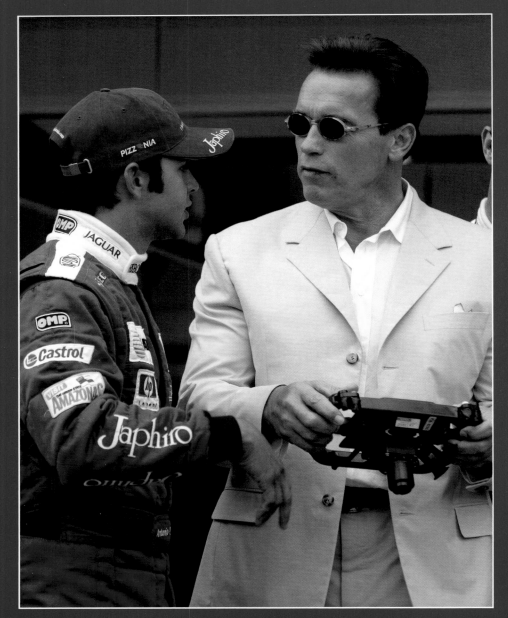

POLE POSITION

2003 RUBENS BARRICHELLO

'90	N. Mansell
'91	N. Mansell
'92	N. Mansell
'93	A. Prost
'94	D. Hill
'95	D. Hill
'96	D. Hill
'97	J. Villeneuve
'98	M. Hakkinen
'99	M. Hakkinen
'00	R. Barrichello
'01	M. Schumacher
'02	J.P. Montoya

2 1 3

	1°	2°	3°
'90	A. Prost	T. Boutsen	A. Senna
'91	N. Mansell	G. Berger	A. Prost
'92	N. Mansell	R. Patrese	M. Brundle
'93	A. Prost	M. Schumacher	R. Patrese
'94	D. Hill	M. Schumacher	J. Alesi
'95	J. Herbert	J. Alesi	D. Coulthard
'96	J. Villeneuve	G. Berger	M. Hakkinen
'97	J. Villeneuve	J. Alesi	A. Wurz
'98	M. Schumacher	M. Hakkinen	E. Irvine
'99	D. Coulthard	E. Irvine	R. Schumacher
'00	D. Coulthard	M. Hakkinen	M. Schumacher
'01	M. Hakkinen	M. Schumacher	R. Barrichello
'02	M. Schumacher	R. Barrichello	J.P. Montoya

STARTING GRID

RUBENS BARRICHELLO
FERRARI
1'21"209

JARNO TRULLI
RENAULT
1'21"381

KIMI RAIKKONEN
MCLAREN
1'21"695

RALF SCHUMACHER
WILLIAMS
1'21"727

MICHAEL SCHUMACHER
FERRARI
1'21"867

CRISTIANO DA MATTA
TOYOTA
1'22"081

JUAN PABLO MONTOYA
WILLIAMS
1'22"214

FERNANDO ALONSO
RENAULT
1'22"404

JACQUES VILLENEUVE
BAR
1'22"591

ANTONIO PIZZONIA
JAGUAR
1'22"634

MARK WEBBER
JAGUAR
1'22"647

DAVID COULTHARD
MCLAREN
1'22"811

OLIVIER PANIS
TOYOTA
1'23"042

H.HARALD FRENTZEN
SAUBER
1'23"187

GIANCARLO FISICHELLA
JORDAN
1'23"574

NICK HEIDFELD
SAUBER
1'23"844

RALPH FIRMAN
JORDAN
1'24"385

JUSTIN WILSON
MINARDI
1'25"468

JOS VERSTAPPEN
MINARDI
1'25"759

JENSON BUTTON
BAR

RESULTS

	DRIVER	CAR	KPH	GAP
1	R. Barrichello	Ferrari	208,757	-
2	J.P. Montoya	Williams	208,543	5"462
3	K. Raikkonen	McLaren	208,339	10"656
4	M. Schumacher	Ferrari	207,755	25"648
5	D. Coulthard	McLaren	207,321	36"827
6	J. Trulli	Renault	207,080	43"067
7	C. Da Matta	Toyota	207,002	45"085
8	J. Button	BAR	206,986	45"478
9	R. Schumacher	Williams	206,503	58"032
10	J. Villeneuve	BAR	206,291	1'03"569
11	O. Panis	Toyota	206,228	1'05"207
12	H.H. Frentzen	Sauber	206,214	1'05"564
13	R. Firman	Jordan	205,248	1 lap
14	M. Webber	Jaguar	205,212	1 lap
15	J. Verstappen	Minardi	201,688	2 laps
16	J. Wilson	Minardi	201,545	2 laps
17	N. Heidfeld	Sauber	201,414	2 laps

RETIREMENTS

F. Alonso	Renault	52	Gearbox
G. Fisichella	Jordan	44	Suspension
A. Pizzonia	Jaguar	32	Engine

THE RACE

DRIVER	LAP	FASTEST LAP	AVERAGE SPEED (KPH)	TOP SPEED
R. Barrichello	38	1'22"236	208,757	259,600
D. Coulthard	60	1'22"692	207,321	262,100
J. Trulli	9	1'22"797	207,080	256,500
F. Alonso	37	1'22"819	205,111	262,200
K. Raikkonen	9	1'22"911	208,339	263,300
J.P. Montoya	33	1'22"938	208,543	262,800
R. Schumacher	10	1'22"943	206,503	266,400
M. Schumacher	10	1'23"024	207,755	260,500
A. Pizzonia	9	1'23"158	198,765	254,500
O. Panis	47	1'23"463	206,228	245,000
C. Da Matta	32	1'23"528	207,002	254,800
J. Villeneuve	57	1'23"705	206,291	254,000
M. Webber	28	1'23"833	205,212	261,600
J. Button	53	1'23"912	206,986	245,400
H.H. Frentzen	58	1'23"933	206,214	245,600
N. Heidfeld	9	1'24"537	201,414	248,900
G. Fisichella	40	1'24"823	198,043	249,400
R. Firman	33	1'25"087	205,248	259,800
J. Wilson	9	1'25"859	201,545	246,100
J. Verstappen	2	1'27"021	201,688	244,800

British GP

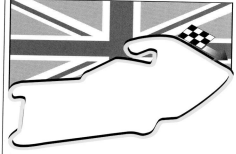

THE CIRCUIT

20 July 2003
Circuit: Silverstone
Km.: 5,141
Laps: 60
Distance: 308,355 Kms

Finally Barrichello!

Silverstone was a spectacular weekend for Rubens, who set pole on Saturday despite starting first on a dirty track with little grip. The Brazilian then went on to dominate the British Grand Prix, despite a poor start that lost him a few places.

At the lights it was Trulli who blasted away first, followed by Raikkonen. For almost ten laps the Italian driver managed to keep the following group at bay, even gaining a couple of seconds on Raikkonen in the McLaren despite the fact that his Renault was clearly slower than his rivals.

But Silverstone was always going to be unpredictable and the fly in the ointment was called Neil Horan, a mentally unstable protestor who ran onto the track on lap 12 with a placard exhorting everyone to read the Bible! Luckily a disaster was averted as Horan proceeded to weave his way between the oncoming cars. Out came the safety-car and everyone came back into the pits together for an unexpected stop.

Trulli also took advantage of the safety car but his Renault was starting to have a few problems. Now Barrichello began his show, picking off Raikkonen for the lead of the race and then passing the backmarkers with a decision that he had never demonstrated during previous races.

In the meantime Schumacher was in difficulty at the back of the field. Even Villeneuve was managing to hold him off, and it was only half-way through the race that the German managed to lap at a decent pace and eventually overtake Trulli to finish fourth.

The podium therefore was made up of a happy and tearful Barrichello, Montoya and Raikkonen, both of whom had driven a colourless race and who were lucky not to have been caught up in the chaotic pit-stops following the track invasion.

HIGHLIGHTS

For the first time in Formula 1 history, a Toyota was in the lead of a grand prix. For 18 laps Da Matta succeeded in heading the field from Raikkonen (McLaren). At the flag the Brazilian finished in seventh, while his team-mate Panis was eleventh after a spell in the leading positions behind Da Matta.

PHOTO PORTFOLIO
PREVIOUS PAGES

Arnold Schwarzenegger pays a visit to Team Jaguar. Two Toyotas were the protagonists of the British GP weekend and Da Matta even led the race for several laps. Winner Rubens Barrichello takes the chequered flag for his first win in 2003 and the sixth in his career.

	CHAMPIONSHIP POINTS	AUSTRALIAN GP	MALAYSIAN GP	BRAZILIAN GP	SAN MARINO GP	SPANISH GP	AUSTRIAN GP	MONACO GP	CANADIAN GP	EUROPEAN GP	FRENCH GP	BRITISH GP	GERMAN GP	HUNGARIAN GP	ITALIAN GP	UNITED STATES GP	JAPANESE GP	TOTAL POINTS
1	M. Schumacher	5	3	-	10	10	10	6	10	4	6	5						69
2	K. Raikkonen	6	10	8	8	-	8	8	3	-	5	6						62
3	J.P. Montoya	8	-	-	2	5	-	10	6	8	8	8						55
4	R. Schumacher	1	5	2	5	4	3	5	8	10	10	-						53
5	R. Barrichello	-	8	-	6	6	6	1	4	6	2	10						49
6	F. Alonso	2	6	6	3	8	-	4	5	5	-	-						39
7	D. Coulthard	10	-	5	4	-	4	2	-	-	4	4						33
8	J. Trulli	4	4	1	-	-	1	3	-	-	-	3						16
9	M. Webber	-	-	-	-	2	2	-	2	3	3	-						12
10	J. Button	-	2	-	1	-	5	-	-	2	-	1						11
11	G. Fisichella	-	-	10	-	-	-	-	-	-	-	-						10
12	H.H. Frentzen	3	-	4	-	-	-	-	-	-	-	-						7
13	C. Da Matta	-	-	-	-	3	-	-	-	-	-	2						5
14	J. Villeneuve	-	-	3	-	-	-	-	-	-	-	-						3
15	N. Heidfeld	-	1	-	-	-	-	-	-	1	-	-						2
16	O. Panis	-	-	-	-	-	-	-	1	-	1	-						2
17	R. Firman	-	-	-	-	1	-	-	-	-	-	-						1
18	A. Pizzonia																	0
19	J. Verstappen																	0
20	J. Wilson																	0

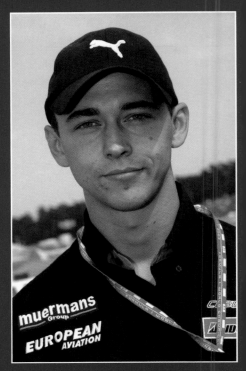

POLE POSITION

2003
JUAN-PABLO MONTOYA

'90	A. Senna
'91	N. Mansell
'92	N. Mansell
'93	A. Prost
'94	G. Berger
'95	D. Hill
'96	D. Hill
'97	G. Berger
'98	M. Hakkinen
'99	M. Hakkinen
'00	D. Coulthard
'01	J.P. Montoya
'02	M. Schumacher

2 1 3

	1°	2°	3°
'90	A. Senna	A. Nannini	G. Berger
'91	N. Mansell	R. Patrese	J. Alesi
'92	N. Mansell	A. Senna	M. Schumacher
'93	A. Prost	M. Schumacher	M. Brundell
'94	G. Berger	O. Panis	E. Bernard
'95	M. Schumacher	D. Coulthard	G. Berger
'96	D. Hill	J. Alesi	J. Villeneuve
'97	G. Berger	M. Schumacher	M. Hakkinen
'98	M. Hakkinen	D. Coulthard	J. Villeneuve
'99	E. Irvine	M. Salo	H.H. Frentzen
'00	R. Barrichello	M. Hakkinen	D. Coulthard
'01	R. Schumacher	R. Barrichello	J. Villeneuve
'02	M. Schumacher	J.P. Montoya	R. Schumacher

STARTING GRID

JUAN PABLO MONTOYA
WILLIAMS
1'15"167

RALF SCHUMACHER
WILLIAMS
1'15"185

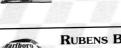

RUBENS BARRICHELLO
FERRARI
1'15"488

JARNO TRULLI
RENAULT
1'15"679

KIMI RAIKKONEN
MCLAREN
1'15"874

MICHAEL SCHUMACHER
FERRARI
1'15"898

OLIVIER PANIS
TOYOTA
1'16"034

FERNANDO ALONSO
RENAULT
1'16"483

CRISTIANO DA MATTA
TOYOTA
1'16"550

DAVID COULTHARD
MCLAREN
1'16"666

MARK WEBBER
JAGUAR
1'16"775

GIANCARLO FISICHELLA
JORDAN
1'16"831

JACQUES VILLENEUVE
BAR
1'17"090

H.HARALD FRENTZEN
SAUBER
1'17"169

NICK HEIDFELD
SAUBER
1'17"557

JUSTIN WILSON
JAGUAR
1'18"021

JENSON BUTTON
BAR
1'18"085

RALPH FIRMAN
JORDAN
1'18"341

JOS VERSTAPPEN
MINARDI
1'19"023

NICOLAS KIESA
MINARDI
1'19"174

RESULTS

	DRIVER	CAR	KPH	GAP
1	J.P. Montoya	Williams	207,036	-
2	D. Coulthard	McLaren	204,523	1'05"459
3	J. Trulli	Renault	204,387	1'09"060
4	F. Alonso	Renault	204,376	1'09"344
5	O. Panis	Toyota	203,372	1 lap
6	C. Da Matta	Toyota	203,196	1 lap
7	M. Schumacher	Ferrari	202,461	1 lap
8	J. Button	BAR	201,128	1 lap
9	J. Villeneuve	BAR	200,311	2 laps
10	N. Heidfeld	Sauber	200,048	2 laps
11	M. Webber	Jaguar	200,923	3 laps
12	N. Kiesa	Minardi	191,143	5 laps
13	G. Fisichella	Jordan	189,491	7 laps

RETIREMENTS

J. Verstappen	Minardi	23	Hydraulic circuit
J. Wilson	Jaguar	6	Transmission
R. Schumacher	Williams	1	Accident
H.H. Frentzen	Sauber	1	Accident
R. Barrichello	Ferrari	0	Accident
K. Raikkonen	McLaren	0	Accident
R. Firman	Jordan	0	Accident

THE RACE

DRIVER	LAP	FASTEST LAP	AVERAGE SPEED (KPH)	TOP SPEED
J.P. Montoya	14	1'14"917	207,036	325,700
J. Trulli	13	1'15"740	204,387	323,000
O. Panis	34	1'15"883	203,372	330,000
D. Coulthard	14	1'16"003	204,523	330,400
C. Da Matta	35	1'16"051	203,196	327,000
F. Alonso	16	1'16"060	204,376	324,800
M. Schumacher	36	1'16"081	202,461	328,900
J. Button	41	1'17"430	201,128	332,400
M. Webber	46	1'17"754	200,923	331,000
N. Heidfeld	10	1'18"036	200,048	324,300
G. Fisichella	51	1'18"145	189,491	324,600
J. Villeneuve	65	1'18"235	200,311	333,300
J. Wilson	3	1'19"441	105,312	316,500
N. Kiesa	26	1'20"171	191,143	318,000
J. Verstappen	6	1'20"399	186,650	317,900
R. Schumacher	-	-	-	-
H.H. Frentzen	-	-	-	-
R. Barrichello	-	-	-	-
K. Raikkonen	-	-	-	-
R. Firman	-	-	-	-

German GP

THE CIRCUIT

3 August 2003
Circuit: Hockenheim
Km.: 4,574
Laps: 67
Distance: 306,458 Kms

Montoya takes a Trulli impressive win!

Montoya dominated the German GP with pole position, fastest lap and his third F1 win, his second this year. The Colombian powered away from the lights in the lead but behind there was chaos. Ralf Schumacher forced Barrichello towards the outside where Raikkonen was trying to get through. The Ferrari driver was boxed in and the three cars made violent contact. For the Brazilian and Raikkonen the race was over, while Ralf also had to retire shortly after.

The safety car came out and on the restart it was the Colombian who got the best start once again, powering away from Trulli and Alonso. Michael Schumacher was fourth, under pressure from Webber and Coulthard. Montoya was out on his own up front and continued to increase his advantage to the point where he could comfortably re-enter the track still in the lead after

his second pit-stop.

The battle was raging behind between the two Renaults, Schumacher in the Ferrari and Coulthard. The German got the better of the other three drivers by overtaking Trulli with twenty laps to go for second place, but he was almost a minute down on Montoya. Ferrari's bad day was not over however. After Barrichello's unfortunate retirement on the opening lap, this time it was Michael who lost second place due to a punctured rear tyre.

After a stop to change tyres, the five-times world champion found himself in seventh place four laps from the end, with no chance of recovering. Montoya took the top podium slot, followed by a consistent Coulthard and Trulli, who beat team-mate Alonso in a sprint finish.

Montoya's sixth successive podium was taking him closer and closer to championship leader Schumacher, who was just six points ahead in the table.

HIGHLIGHTS

Jarno Trulli finished the Hockenheim race totally drained due to a heavy dose of flu over the past few days, which meant that he had to be helped by the medical squad to step up for the podium ceremony.
With third place in the German GP, Trulli has now scored two podium finishes in his career. The first was for Prost in the 1999 European GP.

PHOTO PORTFOLIO
PREVIOUS PAGES

Denmark's Nicolas Kiesa makes his debut for Minardi in place of Justin Wilson, who switches to Jaguar.
On the other page: the incident shortly after the start involving Ralf Schumacher, Raikkonen and Barrichello, and the Finnish driver's McLaren, which was totally destroyed.

	CHAMPIONSHIP POINTS	AUSTRALIAN GP	MALAYSIAN GP	BRAZILIAN GP	SAN MARINO GP	SPANISH GP	AUSTRIAN GP	MONACO GP	CANADIAN GP	EUROPEAN GP	FRENCH GP	BRITISH GP	GERMAN GP	HUNGARIAN GP	ITALIAN GP	UNITED STATES GP	JAPANESE GP	TOTAL POINTS
1	M. Schumacher	5	3	-	10	10	10	6	10	4	6	5	2					71
2	J.P. Montoya	8	-	-	2	5	-	10	6	8	8	8	10					65
3	K. Raikkonen	6	10	8	8	-	8	8	3	-	5	6	-					62
4	R. Schumacher	1	5	2	5	4	3	5	8	10	10	-	-					53
5	R. Barrichello	-	8	-	6	6	6	1	4	6	2	10	-					49
6	F. Alonso	2	6	6	3	8	-	4	5	5	-	-	5					44
7	D. Coulthard	10	-	5	4	-	4	2	-	-	4	4	8					41
8	J. Trulli	4	4	1	-	-	1	3	-	-	-	3	6					22
9	M. Webber	-	-	-	-	2	2	-	2	3	3	-	-					12
10	J. Button	-	2	-	1	-	5	-	-	2	-	1	1					12
11	G. Fisichella	-	-	10	-	-	-	-	-	-	-	-	-					10
12	C. Da Matta	-	-	-	-	3	-	-	-	-	-	2	3					8
13	H.H. Frentzen	3	-	4	-	-	-	-	-	-	-	-	-					7
14	O. Panis	-	-	-	-	-	-	-	1	-	1	-	4					6
15	J. Villeneuve	-	-	3	-	-	-	-	-	-	-	-	-					3
16	N. Heidfeld	-	1	-	-	-	-	-	-	1	-	-	-					2
17	R. Firman	-	-	-	-	1	-	-	-	-	-	-	-					1
18	A. Pizzonia	-	-	-	-	-	-	-	-	-	-	-	-					0
19	J. Verstappen	-	-	-	-	-	-	-	-	-	-	-	-					0
20	J. Wilson	-	-	-	-	-	-	-	-	-	-	-	-					0
21	N. Kiesa	/	/	/	/	/	/	/	/	/	/	/	-					0

193

POLE POSITION

2003 FERNANDO ALONSO

'90	T. Boutsen
'91	A. Senna
'92	R. Patrese
'93	A. Prost
'94	M. Schumacher
'95	D. Hill
'96	M. Schumacher
'97	M. Schumacher
'98	M. Hakkinen
'99	M. Hakkinen
'00	M. Schumacher
'01	M. Schumacher
'02	R. Barrichello

2 1 3

	1°	2°	3°
'90	T. Boutsen	A. Senna	N. Piquet
'91	A. Senna	N. Mansell	R. Patrese
'92	A. Senna	N. Mansell	G. Berger
'93	D. Hill	R. Patrese	G. Berger
'94	M. Schumacher	D. Hill	J. Verstappen
'95	D. Hill	D. Coulthard	G. Berger
'96	J. Villeneuve	D. Hill	J. Alesi
'97	J. Villeneuve	D. Hill	J. Herbert
'98	M. Schumacher	D. Coulthard	J. Villeneuve
'99	M. Hakkinen	D. Coulthard	E. Irvine
'00	M. Hakkinen	M. Schumacher	D. Coulthard
'01	M. Schumacher	R. Barrichello	D. Coulthard
'02	R. Barrichello	M. Schumacher	R. Schumacher

STARTING GRID

FERNANDO ALONSO
RENAULT
1'21"688

RALF SCHUMACHER
WILLIAMS
1'21"944

MARK WEBBER
JAGUAR
1'22"027

JUAN PABLO MONTOYA
WILLIAMS
1'22"180

RUBENS BARRICHELLO
FERRARI
1'22"180

JARNO TRULLI
RENAULT
1'22"610

KIMI RAIKKONEN
McLAREN
1'22"742

MICHAEL SCHUMACHER
FERRARI
1'22"755

DAVID COULTHARD
McLAREN
1'23"060

OLIVIER PANIS
TOYOTA
1'23"369

NICK HEIDFELD
SAUBER
1'23"621

JUSTIN WILSON
JAGUAR
1'23"660

GIANCARLO FISICHELLA
JORDAN
1'23"726

JENSON BUTTON
BAR
1'23"847

CRISTIANO DA MATTA
TOYOTA
1'23"982

JACQUES VILLENEUVE
BAR
1'24"100

H.HARALD FRENTZEN
SAUBER
1'24"569

JOS VERSTAPPEN
MINARDI
1'26"423

ZSOLT BAUMGARTNER
JORDAN
1'26"678

NICOLAS KIESA
MINARDI
1'28"907

RESULTS

	DRIVER	CAR	KPH	GAP
1	F. Alonso	Renault	185,810	-
2	K. Raikkonen	McLaren	185,287	16"768
3	J.P. Montoya	Williams	184,736	34"537
4	R. Schumacher	Williams	184,703	35"620
5	D. Coulthard	McLaren	184,059	56"535
6	M. Webber	Jaguar	183,566	1'02"643
7	J. Trulli	Renault	182,981	1 lap
8	M. Schumacher	Ferrari	182,968	1 lap
9	N. Heidfeld	Sauber	182,237	1 lap
10	J. Button	BAR	181,670	1 lap
11	C. Da Matta	Toyota	179,497	2 laps
12	J. Verstappen	Minardi	176,594	3 laps
13	N. Kiesa	Minardi	173,635	4 laps

RETIREMENTS

H.H. Frentzen	Sauber	47	Fuel pressure
J. Wilson	Jaguar	42	Engine
Z. Baumgartner	Jordan	34	Engine
O. Panis	Toyota	33	Gearbox
G. Fisichella	Jordan	28	Engine
R. Barrichello	Ferrari	19	Suspension
J. Villeneuve	BAR	14	Hydraulic circuit

THE RACE

DRIVER	LAP	FASTEST LAP	AVERAGE SPEED (KPH)	TOP SPEED
J.P. Montoya	37	1'22"095	184,736	305,800
R. Schumacher	55	1'22"319	184,703	307,500
K. Raikkonen	66	1'22"372	185,287	301,300
F. Alonso	47	1'22"565	185,810	292,500
C. Da Matta	36	1'23"040	179,497	303,700
M. Webber	49	1'23"156	183,566	295,700
D. Coulthard	40	1'23"193	184,059	297,400
M. Schumacher	38	1'23"207	182,968	301,200
J. Button	65	1'23"376	181,670	300,200
J. Trulli	34	1'24"100	182,981	292,400
N. Heidfeld	54	1'24"267	182,237	295,700
O. Panis	17	1'24"414	181,523	303,900
H.H. Frentzen	45	1'24"450	181,045	295,800
R. Barrichello	13	1'24"583	180,912	299,500
J. Wilson	26	1'24"936	180,583	297,600
G. Fisichella	13	1'25"081	178,762	297,800
J. Villeneuve	13	1'25"278	176,196	294,600
Z. Baumgartner	22	1'26"464	176,104	291,800
J. Verstappen	60	1'26"559	176,594	292,800
N. Kiesa	47	1'27"641	173,635	290,200

Hungarian GP

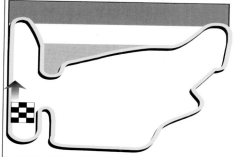

THE CIRCUIT

24 August 2003
Circuit: Hungaroring
Km.: 4,381
Laps: 70
Distance: 306,873 Kms

Sensational maiden win for Alonso!

Right from the start of this year's championship it was clear that sooner or later the talented Spanish youngster Fernando Alonso was going to take Renault back to the winners' circle 20 years after its success with Alain Prost. In Spain Alonso had already come close to taking the win in front of his home crowd, so it was now only a question of time. Add to this the right track – Budapest – which was perfect for the Renault chassis and the Michelin tyres, and the rest is history. Alonso started the weekend well with pole ahead of the two Williams drivers and Webber in the Jaguar, then powered into the lead at an astonishing pace. Webber then held up the chasing group, allowing the Renault driver to increase his advantage to almost 20 seconds by lap 10.

From then on it was just a question of completing the remaining laps to the chequered flag and keeping one eye on engine and tyre performance. The talented Spaniard proved to be a worthy winner, leading the race from lights to flag.

The battle for the remaining places saw Ralf Schumacher, who started from the front row alongside Alonso, spin off at turn 2. Ralf then charged his way back up the field from eighteenth place. On lap 20 he was seventh, on lap 45 he was fifth and one lap later was fourth, a position he would hold until the flag.

On lap 20 the rear suspension broke on Barrichello's Ferrari and he went into the wall, the Brazilian luckily emerging unscathed from the incident. The race ended with victory for Alonso, followed by Raikkonen and Montoya while Schumacher could only finish eighth after a lengthy pit-stop.

HIGHLIGHTS

Who on earth is Zsolt Baumgartner, many seasoned GP observers might have had cause to ask at Budapest.
In the space of a few minutes, the Hungarian F3000 driver and Jordan tester found himself catapulted into Formula 1 as replacement for Ralph Firman, who was still feeling the effects of his crash into the wall during the Saturday morning session.
Baumgartner ran a steady race but retired on lap 34 with engine failure.

PHOTO PORTFOLIO
PREVIOUS PAGES

The double colour page spread is almost entirely dedicated to Renault and its Spanish driver Alonso. Fernando embraces his father and then celebrates with Briatore, who in the last photo raises the team trophy ...... a replica of the Ferrari steering-wheel!

	CHAMPIONSHIP POINTS	AUSTRALIAN GP	MALAYSIAN GP	BRAZILIAN GP	SAN MARINO GP	SPANISH GP	AUSTRIAN GP	MONACO GP	CANADIAN GP	EUROPEAN GP	FRENCH GP	BRITISH GP	GERMAN GP	HUNGARIAN GP	ITALIAN GP	UNITED STATES GP	JAPANESE GP	TOTAL POINTS
1	M. Schumacher	5	3	-	10	10	10	6	10	4	6	5	2	1				72
2	J.P. Montoya	8	-	-	2	5	-	10	6	8	8	8	10	6				71
3	K. Raikkonen	6	10	8	8	-	8	8	3	-	5	6	-	8				70
4	R. Schumacher	1	5	2	5	4	3	5	8	10	10	-	-	5				58
5	F. Alonso	2	6	6	3	8	-	4	5	5	-	-	5	10				54
6	R. Barrichello	-	8	-	6	6	6	1	4	6	2	10	-	-				49
7	D. Coulthard	10	-	5	4	-	4	2	-	-	4	4	8	4				45
8	J. Trulli	4	4	1	-	-	1	3	-	-	-	3	6	2				24
9	M. Webber	-	-	-	-	2	2	-	2	3	3	-	-	3				15
10	J. Button	-	2	-	1	-	5	-	-	2	-	1	1	-				12
11	G. Fisichella	-	-	10	-	-	-	-	-	-	-	-	-	-				10
12	C. Da Matta	-	-	-	-	3	-	-	-	-	-	2	3	-				8
13	H.H. Frentzen	3	-	4	-	-	-	-	-	-	-	-	-	-				7
14	O. Panis	-	-	-	-	-	-	-	1	-	1	-	4	-				6
15	J. Villeneuve	-	-	3	-	-	-	-	-	-	-	-	-	-				3
16	N. Heidfeld	-	1	-	-	-	-	-	1	-	-	-	-	-				2
17	R. Firman	-	-	-	-	1	-	-	-	-	-	-	/	-				1
18	A. Pizzonia	-	-	-	-	-	-	-	-	-	-	/	/	-				0
19	J. Verstappen	-	-	-	-	-	-	-	-	-	-	-	-	-				0
20	J. Wilson	-	-	-	-	-	-	-	-	-	-	-	-	-				0
21	N. Kiesa	/	/	/	/	/	/	/	/	/	/	/	/	/				0
22	Z. Baumgartner	/	/	/	/	/	/	/	/	/	/	/	/					0

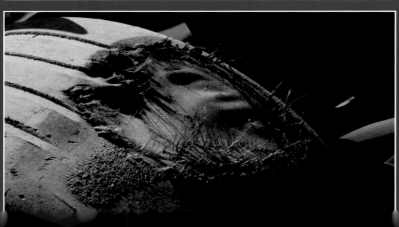

POLE POSITION

2003
MICHAEL
SCHUMACHER

'90	A. Senna
'91	A. Senna
'92	N. Mansell
'93	A. Prost
'94	J. Alesi
'95	D. Coulthard
'96	D. Hill
'97	J. Alesi
'98	M. Schumacher
'99	M. Hakkinen
'00	M. Schumacher
'01	J.P. Montoya
'02	J.P. Montoya

2   **1**   **3**

	1°	2°	3°
'90	A. Senna	A. Prost	G. Berger
'91	N. Mansell	A. Senna	A. Prost
'92	A. Senna	M. Brundle	M. Schumacher
'93	D. Hill	J. Alesi	M. Andretti
'94	D. Hill	G. Berger	M. Hakkinen
'95	J. Herbert	M. Hakkinen	H.H. Frentzen
'96	M. Schumacher	J. Alesi	M. Hakkinen
'97	D. Coulthard	J. Alesi	H.H. Frentzen
'98	M. Schumacher	E. Irvine	R. Schumacher
'99	H.H. Frentzen	R. Schumacher	M. Salo
'00	M. Schumacher	M. Hakkinen	R. Schumacher
'01	J.P. Montoya	R. Barrichello	R. Schumacher
'02	R. Barrichello	M. Schumacher	E. Irvine

STARTING GRID

MICHAEL SCHUMACHER
FERRARI
1'20"963

JUAN PABLO MONTOYA
WILLIAMS
1'21"014

RUBENS BARRICHELLO
FERRARI
1'21"242

KIMI RAIKKONEN
MCLAREN
1'21"466

MARC GENE
WILLIAMS
1'21"834

JARNO TRULLI
RENAULT
1'21"944

JENSON BUTTON
BAR
1'22"301

DAVID COULTHARD
MCLAREN
1'22"471

OLIVIER PANIS
TOYOTA
1'22"488

JACQUES VILLENEUVE
BAR
1'22"717

MARK WEBBER
JAGUAR
1'22"754

CRISTIANO DA MATTA
TOYOTA
1'22"914

GIANCARLO FISICHELLA
JORDAN
1'22"992

H.HARALD FRENTZEN
SAUBER
1'23"216

JUSTIN WILSON
JAGUAR
1'23"484

NICK HEIDFELD
SAUBER
1'23"803

JOS VERSTAPPEN
MINARDI
1'25"078

ZSOLT BAUMGARTNER
JORDAN
1'25"881

NICOLAS KIESA
MINARDI
1'26"778

FERNANDO ALONSO
RENAULT
1'40"405

RESULTS

	DRIVER	CAR	KPH	GAP
1	M. Schumacher	Ferrari	247,585	-
2	J.P. Montoya	Williams	247,292	5"294
3	R. Barrichello	Ferrari	246,930	11"835
4	K. Raikkonen	McLaren	246,875	12"834
5	M. Genè	Williams	246,046	27"891
6	J. Villeneuve	BAR	242,351	1 lap
7	M. Webber	Jaguar	241,457	1 lap
8	F. Alonso	Renault	241,316	1 lap
9	N. Heidfeld	Sauber	241,208	1 lap
10	G. Fisichella	Jordan	238,725	1 lap
11	Z. Baumgartner	Jordan	236,323	2 laps
12	N. Kiesa	Minardi	234,772	2 laps
13	H.H. Frentzen	Sauber	241,611	3 laps

RETIREMENTS

D. Coulthard	McLaren	45	Engine
O. Panis	Toyota	35	Brakes
J. Verstappen	Minardi	27	Hydraulic circuit
J. Button	BAR	24	Gearbox
C. Da Matta	Toyota	3	Wheel
J. Wilson	Jaguar	2	Gearbox
J. Trulli	Renault	0	Engine

THE RACE

DRIVER	LAP	FASTEST LAP	AVERAGE SPEED (KPH)	TOP SPEED
M. Schumacher	14	1'21"832	247,585	368,800
K. Raikkonen	12	1'22"413	246,875	366,300
J.P. Montoya	31	1'22"126	247,292	363,300
R. Barrichello	13	1'22"171	246,930	367,000
M. Gene	12	1'22"413	246,046	367,900
D. Coulthard	10	1'22"427	245,495	364,600
J. Villeneuve	13	1'23"039	242,351	359,600
F. Alonso	47	1'23"195	241,316	357,600
J. Button	13	1'23"225	239,243	362,500
O. Panis	10	1'23"303	234,620	360,000
H.H. Frentzen	14	1'23"518	241,611	359,200
M. Webber	10	1'23"778	241,457	352,000
N. Heidfeld	9	1'24"225	241,208	360,400
G. Fisichella	52	1'25"133	238,725	354,400
Z. Baumgartner	38	1'25"549	236,323	354,300
J. Verstappen	22	1'25"816	220,508	355,800
N. Kiesa	49	1'26"127	234,772	355,100
C. Da Matta	3	1'26"148	230,092	363,500
J. Wilson	2	1'59"265	130,551	343,600
J. Trulli	-	-	-	-

Italian GP

THE CIRCUIT

14 September 2003
Circuit: Monza
Km.: 5,793
Laps: 53
Distance: 306,720 Kms

Schumacher is back with a vengeance!

After five GPs in which Schumacher had only once managed to step onto the podium, and with the media in a frenzy over his poor run of form, the five-times world champion immediately set pole at Monza ahead of his rival Montoya, team-mate Rubens and Raikkonen. Hungarian GP winner Alonso ruined his quick qualifying lap at the first chicane and lined up last on the grid.

Marc Gene, temporary replacement for Ralf Schumacher at Williams who was still recovering from his previous week's crash, set a superb fifth quickest time. At the lights Schummy and Montoya were quick off the mark, but it was Trulli behind who got off to a fantastic start. At the back of the grid Alonso powered away but found the Minardi of Verstappen in his way after the Dutchman had swerved to avoid the

stalled Jaguar of Justin Wilson. The Renault of the Spanish driver flew up and over Verstappen's wheels, destroying its front wing. Both Alonso and the Dutchman had to come into the pits for repairs.

Meanwhile on the opening lap, Montoya attacked Schumacher at the second chicane and made a sensational attempt to pass him round the outside, but the Ferrari driver held firm and the Colombian had to give way. Schumacher held onto the lead amidst the cheers of the crowd and that was the start of his lonely run to the chequered flag. Montoya was penalized with a drive-through penalty for his risky manoeuvre and was then held up by Frentzen while lapping the German, but even so he would never have caught up on Schumacher. Third place went to Barrichello, who did a perfect job as team-mate by taking points away from Schumacher's championship rival, Raikkonen.

HIGHLIGHTS

This time it is the Monza circuit that earns the 'highlights' badge, as Michael Schumacher won the Italian GP at a record pace of almost 250 km/h (247 km/h to be exact), the highest average speed ever recorded in Formula 1. But Monza also saw the highest speed ever reached by a Formula 1 car with more than 368 km/h at the end of the start-finish straight. The previous record was held by Jean Alesi with 363 km/h.

PHOTO PORTFOLIO
PREVIOUS PAGES

Da Matta (Toyota) goes off the track at the Parabolica when his rear tyre punctures. Schumacher raises his hands in triumph in front of the pit-wall, where his mechanics are celebrating the win.

CHAMPIONSHIP POINTS		AUSTRALIAN GP	MALAYSIAN GP	BRAZILIAN GP	SAN MARINO GP	SPANISH GP	AUSTRIAN GP	MONACO GP	CANADIAN GP	EUROPEAN GP	FRENCH GP	BRITISH GP	GERMAN GP	HUNGARIAN GP	ITALIAN GP	UNITED STATES GP	JAPANESE GP	TOTAL POINTS
1	M. Schumacher	5	3	-	10	10	10	6	10	4	6	5	2	1	10			82
2	J.P. Montoya	8	-	-	2	5	-	10	6	8	8	8	10	6	8			79
3	K. Raikkonen	6	10	8	8	-	8	8	3	-	5	6	-	8	5			75
4	R. Schumacher	1	5	2	5	4	3	5	8	10	10	-	-	5	/			58
5	R. Barrichello	-	8	-	6	6	6	1	4	6	2	10	-	-	6			55
6	F. Alonso	2	6	6	3	8	-	4	5	5	-	-	5	10	1			55
7	D. Coulthard	10	-	5	4	-	4	2	-	-	4	4	8	4	-			45
8	J. Trulli	4	4	1	-	-	1	3	-	-	3	6	2	-				24
9	M. Webber	-	-	-	-	2	2	-	2	3	3	-	-	3	2			17
10	J. Button	-	2	-	1	-	5	-	-	2	-	1	1	-	-			12
11	G. Fisichella	-	-	10	-	-	-	-	-	-	-	-	-	-	-			10
12	C. Da Matta	-	-	-	-	3	-	-	-	-	-	2	3	-	-			8
13	H.H. Frentzen	3	-	4	-	-	-	-	-	-	-	-	-	-	-			7
14	O. Panis	-	-	-	-	-	-	-	1	-	1	4	-	-				6
15	J. Villeneuve	-	-	3	-	-	-	-	-	-	-	-	-	-	3			6
16	M. Genè	/	/	/	/	/	/	/	/	/	/	/	/	/	4			4
17	N. Heidfeld	-	1	-	-	-	-	-	-	1	-	-	-	-	-			2
18	R. Firman	-	-	-	-	1	-	-	-	-	-	-	-	/	-			1
19	A. Pizzonia	-	-	-	-	-	-	-	-	-	-	-	/	/	-			0
20	J. Verstappen	-	-	-	-	-	-	-	-	-	-	-	-	-	-			0
21	J. Wilson	-	-	-	-	-	-	-	-	-	-	-	-	-	-			0
22	N. Kiesa	/	/	/	/	/	/	/	/	/	/	/	/	/	-			0
23	Z. Baumgartner	/	/	/	/	/	/	/	/	/	/	/	/	/	-			0

POLE POSITION

2003
KIMI RAIKKONEN

'00 M. Schumacher
'01 M. Schumacher
'02 M. Schumacher

	2	1	3	
	1°	2°	3°

	1°	2°	3°
'00	M. Schumacher	R. Barrichello	H.H. Frentzen
'01	M. Hakkinen	M. Schumacher	D. Coulthard
'02	R. Barrichello	M. Schumacher	D. Coulthard

STARTING GRID

KIMI RAIKKONEN
MCLAREN
1'11"670

RUBENS BARRICHELLO
FERRARI
1'11"794

OLIVIER PANIS
TOYOTA
1'11"920

JUAN PABLO MONTOYA
WILLIAMS
1'11"948

RALF SCHUMACHER
WILLIAMS
1'12"078

FERNANDO ALONSO
RENAULT
1'12"087

MICHAEL SCHUMACHER
FERRARI
1'12"194

DAVID COULTHARD
MCLAREN
1'12"297

CRISTIANO DA MATTA
TOYOTA
1'12"326

JARNO TRULLI
RENAULT
1'12"566

JENSON BUTTON
BAR
1'12"695

JACQUES VILLENEUVE
BAR
1'13"050

NICK HEIDFELD
SAUBER
1'13"083

MARK WEBBER
JAGUAR
1'13"269

H. HARALD FRENTZEN
SAUBER
1'13"447

JUSTIN WILSON
JAGUAR
1'13"585

GIANCARLO FISICHELLA
JORDAN
1'13"798

RALPH FIRMAN
JORDAN
1'14"027

JOS VERSTAPPEN
MINARDI
1'15"360

NICOLAS KIESA
MINARDI
1'15"644

RESULTS

	DRIVER	CAR	KPH	GAP
1	M. Schumacher	Ferrari	196,164	-
2	K. Raikkonen	McLaren	195,528	18"258
3	H.H. Frentzen	Sauber	194,847	37"964
4	J. Trulli	Renault	194,490	48"329
5	N. Heidfeld	Sauber	194,213	56"403
6	J.P. Montoya	Williams	191,159	1 lap
7	G. Fisichella	Jordan	191,114	1 lap
8	J. Wilson	Jaguar	189,631	2 laps
9	C. Da Matta	Toyota	188,372	2 laps
10	J. Verstappen	Minardi	185,384	4 laps
11	N. Kiesa	Minardi	183,863	4 laps

RETIREMENTS

J. Villeneuve	BAR	63	Engine
R. Firman	Jordan	48	Crashed
D. Coulthard	McLaren	45	Transmission
F. Alonso	Renault	44	Engine
J. Button	BAR	41	Engine
O. Panis	Toyota	27	Crashed
M. Webber	Jaguar	21	Crashed
R. Schumacher	Williams	21	Crashed
R. Barrichello	Ferrari	2	Accident

THE RACE

DRIVER	LAP	FASTEST LAP	AVERAGE SPEED (KPH)	TOP SPEED
M. Schumacher	13	1'11"473	196,164	355,700
F. Alonso	9	1'11"525	187,711	347,100
J.P. Montoya	9	1'11"595	191,159	358,900
K. Raikkonen	9	1'11"617	195,528	346,700
R. Schumacher	13	1'11"655	199,076	352,800
D. Coulthard	12	1'12"009	180,640	349,500
J. Trulli	14	1'12"015	194,490	351,200
J. Button	10	1'13"038	192,623	349,100
N. Heidfeld	13	1'13"085	194,213	342,000
M. Webber	12	1'13"099	200,418	345,900
C. Da Matta	13	1'13"231	188,372	341,700
J. Wilson	12	1'13"324	189,631	346,700
H.H. Frentzen	71	1'13"338	194,847	342,200
O. Panis	12	1'13"340	178,005	339,000
J. Villeneuve	62	1'13"538	186,668	344,100
G. Fisichella	13	1'13"630	191,114	335,800
R. Barrichello	2	1'13"905	193,782	349,900
R. Firman	11	1'14"687	178,412	337,600
N. Kiesa	67	1'14"737	183,863	338,500
J. Verstappen	68	1'15"257	185,384	339,900

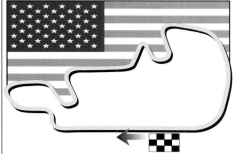

United States GP

THE CIRCUIT

28 September 2003
Circuit: Indianapolis
Km.: 4,192
Laps: 73
Distance: 306,016 Kms

Schumacher's masterful race!

This year Ferrari's German driver has given his fans cause to worry on many occasions, but when it comes to the crunch he has always demonstrated that he is still the king of F1.
In the races before Monza and in Indianapolis qualifying Schumacher appeared to be tired and off-form, relegated to the secondary grid positions and incapable of squaring up to his rivals.
Then came a flash of genius: at Monza with pole position and a win. At Indianapolis he was only seventh in qualifying but this was followed by a fantastic victory and a major step forward towards the world title.
Pole went to Kimi Raikkonen followed by Barrichello, who has often been faster than Schumacher in qualifying this year, and a superb Panis (Toyota) who qualified ahead of the two Williams. At the lights Michael made a great start and immediately rocketed up to fourth place while Montoya was strangely passed by two cars and slipped into

the middle of the the midfield runners. It looked as if Raikkonen was going to have things all his own way because it soon began to rain and Schumacher was suddenly in difficulty with his tyres, the German losing several positions. Montoya, aware that his title hopes were slipping away, began to attack Barrichello but recklessly lunged past the Brazilian, sending him spinning into the gravel. The Colombian would eventually be hit with a drive-through penalty, which together with a 15 second pit-stop due to fuel rig failure, cost him the race and the title.
In the meantime the rain showers and the frenetic pit-stops upset team strategies and the standings. Only Schumacher kept a cool head and the German caught and then took Raikkonen to power towards a fantastic victory. Third was an incredulous Frentzen (Sauber), who said farewell to Formula 1 in the best possible way, followed by Trulli, Heidfeld in the second Swiss car and Montoya. Fisichella also finished in the points as did Wilson (Jaguar) for the first time in his career.

HIGHLIGHTS

The title of 'Driver of the Day' must go to Heinz-Harald Frentzen. The 36 year-old German, in his tenth season in Formula 1, is one of the 'veterans' of grand prix racing. This year will probably be his last season in F1, as he decides to retire after 157 races and 3 wins; one in 1997 at Imola with Williams and two in 1999 with Jordan.

PHOTO PORTFOLIO
PREVIOUS PAGES

The exciting Indianapolis weekend. Schummy stopped at the side of the track in Saturday qualifying, followed by Barrichello's retirement in the race, the pit-stop chaos due to the rain and Schumacher's triumphant arrival.

	CHAMPIONSHIP POINTS	AUSTRALIAN GP	MALAYSIAN GP	BRAZILIAN GP	SAN MARINO GP	SPANISH GP	AUSTRIAN GP	MONACO GP	CANADIAN GP	EUROPEAN GP	FRENCH GP	BRITISH GP	GERMAN GP	HUNGARIAN GP	ITALIAN GP	UNITED STATES GP	JAPANESE GP	TOTAL POINTS
1	M. Schumacher	5	3	-	10	10	10	6	10	4	6	5	2	1	10	10		92
2	K. Raikkonen	6	10	8	8	-	8	8	3	-	5	6	-	8	5	8		83
3	J.P. Montoya	8	-	-	2	5	-	10	6	8	8	8	10	6	8	3		82
4	R. Schumacher	1	5	2	5	4	3	5	8	10	10	-	-	5	/	-		58
5	R. Barrichello	-	8	-	6	6	6	1	4	6	2	10	-	-	6	-		55
6	F. Alonso	2	6	6	3	8	-	4	5	5	-	-	5	10	1	-		55
7	D. Coulthard	10	-	5	4	-	4	2	-	-	4	4	8	4	-	-		45
8	J. Trulli	4	4	1	-	-	1	3	-	-	-	3	6	2	-	5		29
9	M. Webber	-	-	-	-	2	2	-	2	3	3	-	-	3	2	-		17
10	H.H. Frentzen	3	-	4	-	-	-	-	-	-	-	-	-	-	-	6		13
11	J. Button	-	2	-	1	-	5	-	-	2	-	1	1	-	-	-		12
12	G. Fisichella	-	-	10	-	-	-	-	-	-	-	-	-	-	-	2		12
13	C. Da Matta	-	-	-	-	3	-	-	-	-	-	2	3	-	-	-		8
14	N. Heidfeld	-	1	-	-	-	-	-	-	1	-	-	-	-	-	4		6
15	O. Panis	-	-	-	-	-	-	1	-	1	-	4	-	-	-	-		6
16	J. Villeneuve	-	-	3	-	-	-	-	-	-	-	-	-	-	3	-		6
17	M. Genè	/	/	/	/	/	/	/	/	/	/	/	/	/	4	-		4
18	R. Firman	-	-	-	-	1	-	-	-	-	-	-	-	/	-	-		1
19	J. Wilson	-	-	-	-	-	-	-	-	-	-	-	-	-	1	-		1
20	A. Pizzonia	-	-	-	-	-	-	-	-	-	-	-	/	/	-	-		0
21	J. Verstappen	-	-	-	-	-	-	-	-	-	-	-	-	-	-	-		0
22	N. Kiesa	/	/	/	/	/	/	/	/	/	/	/	/	-	-	-		0
23	Z. Baumgartner	/	/	/	/	/	/	/	/	/	/	/	-	-	-	/		0

POLE POSITION

2003 RUBENS BARRICHELLO

'90	A. Senna
'91	G. Berger
'92	N. Mansell
'93	A. Prost
'94	M. Schumacher
'95	M. Schumacher
'96	J. Villeneuve
'97	J. Villeneuve
'98	M. Schumacher
'99	M. Schumacher
'00	M. Schumacher
'01	M. Schumacher
'02	M. Schumacher

2   **1**   **3**

	1°	2°	3°
'90	N. Piquet	R. Moreno	A. Suzuki
'91	G. Berger	A. Senna	R. Patrese
'92	R. Patrese	G. Berger	M. Brundle
'93	A. Senna	A. Prost	M. Hakkinen
'94	D. Hill	M. Schumacher	J. Alesi
'95	M. Schumacher	M. Hakkinen	J. Herbert
'96	D. Hill	M. Schumacher	M. Hakkinen
'97	M. Schumacher	H.H. Frentzen	E. Irvine
'98	M. Hakkinen	E. Irvine	D. Coulthard
'99	M. Hakkinen	M. Schumacher	E. Irvine
'00	M. Schumacher	M. Hakkinen	D. Coulthard
'01	M. Schumacher	J.P. Montoya	D. Coulthard
'02	M. Schumacher	R. Barrichello	K. Raikkonen

STARTING GRID

 RUBENS BARRICHELLO
FERRARI
1'31"713

 JUAN PABLO MONTOYA
WILLIAMS
1'32"412

 CRISTIANO DA MATTA
TOYOTA
1'32"419

 OLIVIER PANIS
TOYOTA
1'32"862

 FERNANDO ALONSO
RENAULT
1'33"044

 MARK WEBBER
JAGUAR
1'33"106

 DAVID COULTHARD
MCLAREN
1'33"137

 KIMI RAIKKONEN
MCLAREN
1'33"272

 JENSON BUTTON
BAR
1'33"474

 JUSTIN WILSON
JAGUAR
1'33"558

 NICK HEIDFELD
SAUBER
1'33"632

 H.HARALD FRENTZEN
SAUBER
1'33"896

 TAKUMA SATO
BAR
1'33"924

 MICHAEL SCHUMACHER
FERRARI
1'34"302

 RALPH FIRMAN
JORDAN
1'34"771

 GIANCARLO FISICHELLA
JORDAN
1'34"912

 JOS VERSTAPPEN
MINARDI
1'34"975

 NICOLAS KIESA
MINARDI
1'37"226

 JARNO TRULLI
RENAULT

RALF SCHUMACHER
WILLIAMS

RESULTS

	DRIVER	CAR	KPH	GAP
1	R. Barrichello	Ferrari	216,611	-
2	K. Raikkonen	McLaren	216,142	11"085
3	D. Coulthard	McLaren	216,120	11"614
4	J. Button	BAR	215,217	33"106
5	J. Trulli	Renault	215,169	34"269
6	T. Sato	BAR	214,443	51"692
7	C. Da Matta	Toyota	214,231	56"794
8	M. Schumacher	Ferrari	214,119	59"487
9	N: Heidfeld	Sauber	214,091	1'00"159
10	O. Panis	Toyota	214,022	1'01"844
11	M. Webber	Jaguar	213,643	1'11"005
12	R. Schumacher	Williams	212,496	1 lap
13	J. Wilson	Jaguar	211,230	1 lap
14	R. Firman	Jordan	208,064	2 laps
15	J. Verstappen	Minardi	206,477	2 laps
16	N. Kiesa	Minardi	203,960	3 laps

RETIREMENTS

G. Fisichella	Jordan	33	Fuel pressure
F. Alonso	Renault	17	Engine
H.H. Frentzen	Sauber	9	Engine
J.P. Montoya	Williams	9	Hydraulic circuit

THE RACE

DRIVER	LAP	FASTEST LAP	AVERAGE SPEED (KPH)	TOP SPEED
R. Schumacher	43	1'33"408	212,496	306,400
D. Coulthard	14	1'33"416	216,120	309,900
M. Schumacher	14	1'33"553	214,119	315,000
R. Barrichello	18	1'33"703	216,611	299,700
J.P. Montoya	2	1'33"830	202,918	301,700
F. Alonso	8	1'34"255	215,467	306,900
K. Raikkonen	12	1'34"488	216,142	304,200
J. Trulli	26	1'34"546	215,169	297,600
J. Button	14	1'34"605	215,217	302,300
M. Webber	24	1'34"635	213,643	297,600
N. Heidfeld	31	1'34"991	214,091	301,500
J. Wilson	11	1'35"014	211,230	303,200
O. Panis	53	1'35"023	214,022	301,100
C. Da Matta	16	1'35"192	214,231	306,700
T. Sato	28	1'35"290	214,443	304,700
G. Fisichella	33	1'35"824	212,113	298,800
H.H. Frentzen	7	1'36"601	204,453	293,200
R. Firman	15	1'36"662	208,064	291,700
J. Verstappen	51	1'37"869	206,477	288,700
N. Kiesa	6	1'38"754	203,960	287,500

Japanese GP

THE CIRCUIT

12 October 2003
Circuit: Suzuka
Km.: 5,807
Laps: 53
Distance: 307,573 Kms

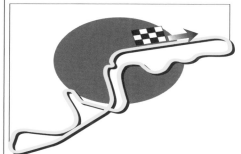

Barrichello takes final win for Ferrari

Never in the history of F1 had a team succeeded in winning five successive world titles, while Schumacher overtook Juan Manuel Fangio's record of five drivers' titles when he won his sixth championship this year. But 2003's triumph also bore the name of Barrichello, whose win in the final GP of the year in Japan ensured that his German team-mate clinched the title. Rubens was the star of the Suzuka weekend, first with pole position on Saturday and then with a fantastic flawless race that left Raikkonen with no possibility of victory as the Finnish driver could still have taken the title with the maximum points. Only the retirement of the Brazilian's Ferrari could have caused problems for Schumacher but it was not to be. What about Schumacher's weekend? It began badly with 14th place on the grid, thanks also to a wet track on his quick lap and it continued with a nervous race in which his sole aim was to reach the eighth place that would guarantee him his sixth world title. All this tension and nervousness twice almost proved to be his downfall. On lap 6 in fact Schumacher made contact with the BAR of Sato who was returning to the track and the German had to enter the pits with a damaged front wing. Then at the end of the race he almost crashed again, this time with his brother, who suddenly moved sideways to avoid hitting Da Matta. But these were the last moments of tension as Barrichello cruised to the win, followed by Raikkonen and Coulthard, Button in the BAR, Trulli in the Renault and surprisingly, the other BAR of Japanese driver Sato, who was hauled in the air in triumph by the team.

Schummy was eighth behind Da Matta in the Toyota and despite this modest result, the German went on to celebrate the conquest of his record-breaking titles with the other members of his team.

HIGHLIGHTS

After 132 GPs and a world title in 1997 with Williams-Renault, Jacques Villeneuve did not take part in the Suzuka race because just a few days earlier the Canadian had terminated his rapport with BAR.
He was replaced by Japanese driver Sato, the team's test driver. Ironically, both BARs finished in the points in Japan for the first time this year.

PHOTO PORTFOLIO
PREVIOUS PAGES

Celebrations for BAR-Honda and Sato at their home circuit with sixth place. Schumacher had a couple of critical moments: first a broken front wing and then a battle with Da Matta and his brother Ralf. Finally Barrichello's triumph and celebrating with Schumacher.

	CHAMPIONSHIP POINTS	AUSTRALIAN GP	MALAYSIAN GP	BRAZILIAN GP	SAN MARINO GP	SPANISH GP	AUSTRIAN GP	MONACO GP	CANADIAN GP	EUROPEAN GP	FRENCH GP	BRITISH GP	GERMAN GP	HUNGARIAN GP	ITALIAN GP	UNITED STATES GP	JAPANESE GP	TOTAL POINTS
1	M. Schumacher	5	3	-	10	10	10	6	10	4	6	5	2	1	10	10	1	93
2	K. Raikkonen	6	10	8	8	-	8	8	3	-	5	6	-	8	5	8	8	91
3	J.P. Montoya	8	-	-	2	5	-	10	6	8	8	8	10	6	8	3	-	82
4	R. Barrichello	-	8	-	6	6	6	1	4	6	2	10	-	-	6	-	10	65
5	R. Schumacher	1	5	2	5	4	3	5	8	10	10	-	-	5	/	-	-	58
6	F. Alonso	2	6	6	3	8	-	4	5	5	-	-	5	10	1	-	-	55
7	D. Coulthard	10	-	5	4	-	4	2	-	-	4	4	8	4	-	-	6	51
8	J. Trulli	4	4	1	-	-	1	3	-	-	-	3	6	2	-	5	4	33
9	J. Button	-	2	-	1	-	5	-	-	2	-	1	1	-	-	-	5	17
10	M. Webber	-	-	-	-	2	2	-	2	3	3	-	-	3	2	-	-	17
11	H.H. Frentzen	3	-	4	-	-	-	-	-	-	-	-	-	-	-	6	-	13
12	G. Fisichella	-	-	10	-	-	-	-	-	-	-	-	-	-	-	2	-	12
13	C. Da Matta	-	-	-	-	3	-	-	-	-	-	2	3	-	-	-	2	10
14	N. Heidfeld	-	1	-	-	-	-	-	-	1	-	-	-	-	-	4	-	6
15	O. Panis	-	-	-	-	-	-	1	-	1	-	4	-	-	-	-	-	6
16	J. Villeneuve	-	-	3	-	-	-	-	-	-	-	-	-	-	3	-	/	6
17	M. Genè	/	/	/	/	/	/	/	/	/	/	/	/	/	4	-	/	4
18	T. Sato	/	/	/	/	/	/	/	/	/	/	/	/	/	/	-	3	3
19	R. Firman	-	-	-	-	1	-	-	-	-	-	-	-	-	/	-	-	1
20	J. Wilson	-	-	-	-	-	-	-	-	-	-	-	-	-	-	1	-	1
21	A. Pizzonia	-	-	-	-	-	-	-	-	-	-	-	-	/	-	-	-	0
22	J. Verstappen	-	-	-	-	-	-	-	-	-	-	-	-	-	-	-	-	0
23	N. Kiesa	/	/	/	/	/	/	/	/	/	/	/	/	/	-	-	-	0
24	Z. Baumgartner	/	/	/	/	/	/	/	/	/	/	/	/	/	-	-	/	0

2003 World Championship: Drivers & Constructors

Drivers

Drivers	Australian GP	Malaysian GP	Brazilian GP	San Marino GP	Spanish GP	Austrian GP	Monaco GP	Canadian GP	European GP	French GP	British GP	German GP	Hungarian GP	Italian GP	United States GP	Japanese GP	Total Points
M. Schumacher	5	3	-	10	10	10	6	10	4	6	5	2	1	10	10	1	93
K. Raikkonen	6	10	8	8	-	8	8	3	-	5	6	-	8	5	8	8	91
J.P. Montoya	8	-	-	2	5	-	10	6	8	8	8	10	6	8	3	-	82
R. Barrichello	-	8	-	6	6	6	1	4	6	2	10	-	-	6	-	10	65
R. Schumacher	1	5	2	5	4	3	5	8	10	10	-	-	5	-	-	-	58
F. Alonso	2	6	6	3	8	-	4	5	5	-	-	5	10	1	-	-	55
D. Coulthard	10	-	5	4	-	4	2	-	-	4	4	8	4	-	-	6	51
J. Trulli	4	4	1	-	-	1	3	-	-	-	3	6	2	-	5	4	33
J. Button	-	2	-	1	-	5	-	-	2	-	1	1	-	-	-	5	17
M. Webber	-	-	-	2	2	-	2	3	3	-	-	3	2	-	-	-	17
H.H. Frentzen	3	-	4	-	-	-	-	-	-	-	-	-	-	-	6	-	13
G. Fisichella	-	-	10	-	-	-	-	-	-	-	-	-	-	2	-	-	12
C. Da Matta	-	-	-	-	3	-	-	-	-	-	2	3	-	-	-	2	10
N. Heidfeld	-	1	-	-	-	-	-	1	-	-	-	-	-	-	4	-	6
O. Panis	-	-	-	-	-	-	1	-	1	-	4	-	-	-	-	-	6
J. Villeneuve	-	-	3	-	-	-	-	-	-	-	-	-	-	3	-	-	6
M. Gene	-	-	-	-	-	-	-	-	-	-	-	-	-	4	-	-	4
T. Sato	-	-	-	-	-	-	-	-	-	-	-	-	-	-	-	3	3
R. Firman	-	-	-	1	-	-	-	-	-	-	-	-	-	-	-	-	1
J. Wilson	-	-	-	-	-	-	-	-	-	-	-	-	-	-	1	-	1

Constructors

Constructors	Australian GP	Malaysian GP	Brazilian GP	San Marino GP	Spanish GP	Austrian GP	Monaco GP	Canadian GP	European GP	French GP	British GP	German GP	Hungarian GP	Italian GP	United States GP	Japanese GP	Total Points
Ferrari	5	11	-	16	16	16	7	14	10	8	15	2	1	16	10	11	158
Williams	9	5	2	7	9	3	15	14	18	18	8	10	11	12	3	-	144
McLaren	16	10	13	12	-	12	10	3	-	9	10	8	12	5	8	14	142
Renault	6	10	7	3	8	1	7	5	5	-	3	11	12	1	5	4	88
BAR	-	2	3	1	-	5	-	-	2	-	1	1	-	3	-	8	26
Sauber	3	1	4	-	-	-	-	1	-	-	-	-	-	-	10	-	19
Jaguar	-	-	-	2	2	-	2	3	3	-	-	3	2	1	-	-	18
Toyota	-	-	-	-	3	-	1	-	1	-	6	3	-	-	-	2	16
Jordan	-	-	10	1	-	-	-	-	-	-	-	-	-	2	-	-	13

Results

Driver	N° GP	N° Pole Position	N° Fastest Lap	N° Retirements	Australian GP	Malaysian GP	Brazilian GP	San Marino GP	Spanish GP	Austrian GP	Monaco GP	Canadian GP	European GP	French GP	British GP	German GP	Hungarian GP	Italian GP	United States GP	Japanese GP
M. Schumacher	16	5	5	1	4	6	R	1	1	1	3	1	5	3	4	7	8	1	1	8
K. Raikkonen	16	2	3	3	3	1	2	2	R	2	2	6	R	4	3	R	2	4	2	2
J.P. Montoya	16	1	3	3	2	12	R	7	4	R	1	3	2	2	2	1	3	2	6	R
R. Barrichello	16	3	3	5	R	2	R	3	3	3	8	5	3	7	1	R	R	3	R	1
R. Schumacher	15	3	1	2	8	4	7	4	5	6	4	2	1	1	9	R	4	-	R	12
F. Alonso	16	2	1	5	7	3	3	6	2	R	5	4	4	R	R	4	1	8	R	R
D. Coulthard	16	-	-	5	1	R	4	6	R	5	7	R	15	5	5	2	5	R	R	3
J. Trulli	16	-	-	5	5	5	8	13	R	8	6	R	R	R	6	3	7	R	4	5
J. Button	15	-	-	5	10	7	R	8	9	4	-	R	7	R	8	8	10	R	R	4
M. Webber	16	-	-	5	R	R	9	7	7	R	7	6	6	14	11	6	7	R	11	R
H.H. Frentzen	16	-	-	7	6	9	5	11	R	R	R	9	12	12	R	13	R	R	3	R
G. Fisichella	16	-	-	8	12	R	1	15	R	R	10	R	12	R	13	R	10	7	R	R
C. Da Matta	16	-	-	3	R	11	10	12	6	10	9	11	R	11	7	6	11	R	9	7
N. Heidfeld	16	-	-	4	R	8	R	10	R	11	R	8	13	17	10	9	9	9	5	9
O. Panis	16	-	-	9	R	R	R	9	R	13	8	R	8	11	5	R	R	R	R	10
J. Villeneuve	15	-	-	8	9	R	6	R	R	12	R	R	R	9	10	9	R	6	R	-
M. Gene	1	-	-	-	-	-	-	-	-	-	-	-	-	-	-	-	-	5	-	-
T. Sato	1	-	-	-	-	-	-	-	-	-	-	-	-	-	-	-	-	-	-	6
R. Firman	15	-	-	7	R	10	R	8	11	12	R	11	15	13	R	R	-	R	-	14
J. Wilson	16	-	-	9	R	R	R	11	13	R	13	14	16	R	R	R	R	R	8	13

R: retired

World Champions 1950-2003

Driver	Car	Year	Constructor
N. Farina	(I - Alfa Romeo)	1950	
J.M. Fangio	(RA - Alfa Romeo)	1951	
A. Ascari	(I - Ferrari)	1952	
A. Ascari	(I - Ferrari)	1953	
J.M. Fangio	(RA - Maserati, Mercedes)	1954	
J.M. Fangio	(RA - Mercedes)	1955	
J.M. Fangio	(RA - Ferrari)	1956	
J.M. Fangio	(RA - Maserati)	1957	
M. Hawthorn	(GB - Ferrari)	1958	Vanwall
J. Brabham	(AUS - Cooper)	1959	Cooper
J. Brabham	(AUS - Cooper)	1960	Cooper
P. Hill	(USA - Ferrari)	1961	Ferrari
G. Hill	(GB - Brm)	1962	Brm
J. Clark	(GB - Lotus)	1963	Lotus
J. Surtees	(GB - Ferrari)	1964	Ferrari
J. Clark	(GB - Lotus)	1965	Lotus
J. Brabham	(AUS - Brabham)	1966	Brabham
D. Hulme	(NZ - Brabham)	1967	Brabham
G. Hill	(GB - Lotus)	1968	Lotus
J. Stewart	(GB - Matra)	1969	Matra
J. Rindt	(A - Lotus)	1970	Lotus
J. Stewart	(GB - Tyrrell)	1971	Tyrrell
E. Fittipaldi	(BR - Lotus)	1972	Lotus
J. Stewart	(GB - Tyrrell)	1973	Tyrrell
E. Fittipaldi	(BR - McLaren)	1974	McLaren
N. Lauda	(A - Ferrari)	1975	Ferrari
J. Hunt	(GB - McLaren)	1976	Ferrari
N. Lauda	(A - Ferrari)	1977	Ferrari
M. Andretti	(USA - Lotus)	1978	Lotus
J. Scheckter	(ZA - Ferrari)	1979	Ferrari
A. Jones	(AUS - Williams)	1980	Williams
N. Piquet	(BR - Brabham)	1981	Williams
K. Rosberg	(SF - Williams)	1982	Ferrari
N. Piquet	(BR - Brabham)	1983	Ferrari
N. Lauda	(A - McLaren)	1984	McLaren
A. Prost	(F - McLaren)	1985	McLaren
A. Prost	(F - McLaren)	1986	Williams
N. Piquet	(BR - Williams)	1987	Williams
A. Senna	(BR - McLaren)	1988	McLaren
A. Prost	(F - McLaren)	1989	McLaren
A. Senna	(BR - McLaren)	1990	McLaren
A. Senna	(BR - McLaren)	1991	McLaren
N. Mansell	(GB - Williams)	1992	Williams
A. Prost	(F - Williams)	1993	Williams
M. Schumacher	(D - Benetton)	1994	Williams
M. Schumacher	(D - Benetton)	1995	Benetton
D. Hill	(GB - Williams)	1996	Williams
J. Villeneuve	(CDN - Williams)	1997	Williams
M. Hakkinen	(FIN - McLaren)	1998	McLaren
M. Hakkinen	(FIN - McLaren)	1999	Ferrari
M. Schumacher	(D - Ferrari)	2000	Ferrari
M. Schumacher	(D - Ferrari)	2001	Ferrari
M. Schumacher	(D - Ferrari)	2002	Ferrari
M. Schumacher	(D - Ferrari)	2003	Ferrari